Vietnam:
Perspectives
& Performance

Vietnam: Perspectives & Performance

Two plays about real people affected by the legacy of the Vietnam Conflict, told in their own words from their own experiences

IOWA STORIES: THE VIETNAM EXPERIENCE
by
Marilyn Shaw

&

VIETNAMESE CHESS
by
Chris Ellsbury & Jennifer Terry

Introduction by Phyllis Carlin, Ph.D

Published by
The Association for Textual Study and Production
Department of English Language and Literature
University of Northern Iowa
Cedar Falls, Iowa

The Association for Textual Study and Production

Director/General Editor: Mary Rohrberger
Assoc. Director/Series Editor: Noel Harold Kaylor, Jr.
Text Designer: Chris Ellsbury
Cover Designer: Osie Johnson, Jr.

Northern Iowa Texts, No. 1
Second Edition

Vietnam: Perspectives and Performance Copyright 1996 by the Association for Textual Study and Production.

ISBN # 0-9641511-3-8

All rights reserved. No part of this book may be reproduced, stored in a retrieval system, or transmitted by any form or by any means, electronic, mechanical, photocopying, recording, or otherwise, except as may be expressly permitted by the applicable copyright statutes, or in writing by the publisher. For specific rights and regulations for *Iowa Stories: The Vietnam Experience* and *Vietnamese Chess*, please contact:

The Association for Textual Study and Production
Department of English Language and Literature
Baker 115, University of Northern Iowa
Cedar Falls, Iowa 50614-0502
(319) 273-2821

Findings, conclusions, and opinions expressed in *Vietnam: Perspectives and Performance* do not necessarily represent the view of the Iowa Humanities Board nor the National Endowment for the Humanities.

This volume is dedicated to all the Vietnam veterans and spouses who shared themselves with us in these oral history projects and all the Vietnam veterans and their families across Iowa and the United States.

Foreword

Perspective is a powerful word. It reminds us that nothing is one-dimensional. Everything has angles, views, sides, strengths, weaknesses, hidden facets, etc., and no one representation of a person, place, thing, or event can depict it with complete accuracy. A corollary to this is the knowledge that every individual is unique. We all have combinations of experiences which have molded our understanding of the world in distinct ways.

Because of this, we are often counseled "to look at it in a different way" or "to see it in another light" or "to judge others only after walking a mile in their shoes." We have an obligation to seek out new perspectives because it is from them that we may understand more fully the issues at hand.

VIETNAM: PERSPECTIVES AND PERFORMANCE attempts to bring to light the experiences of Vietnam veterans and their spouses, not in the words of a Hollywood screenwriter, but in the actual words of the people who lived the stories which are told. The scripts have sought to recognize similarities as well as differences in the experiences of those Americans whose lives have been affected by our nation's involvement in the Vietnam Conflict.

To appreciate their stories, their histories, you as reader must allow yourself to abandon, for a time, any preconceived notions of what Vietnam was and is, and take on for the moment the perspectives of the characters presented. Do not attempt to integrate their understanding of the war into yours as you read. Instead, try to create a picture of their understanding first, and only afterward process it with your own views. By distancing your own experiences from those in the scripts, new and important perspectives of the Vietnam legacy may be revealed to you.

CHRIS ELLSBURY
JUNE 1993

Acknowledgements

This book could not have been accomplished without the support, encouragement, funding, and expertise of the following individuals and organizations, and the authors are greatly indebted to them for their assistance: The University of Northern Iowa Departments of: Communication Studies • English Language and Literature • Theatre • Information Systems and Computing Services • Office of Academic Affairs • College of Humanities and Fine Arts • Graduate College • Grants & Contracts Office • Office of Public Relations • Affirmative Action Office • UNI Foundation • National Endowment for the Humanities • Iowa Humanities Board • Office of Senator Charles Grassley • Britt Small and Festival • National Bank of Waterloo • Veterans Committee of UAW Local 838 • Waterloo Streets Department • Dean Beverley Byers-Pevitts • Dr. Phyllis Carlin • Dr. April Chatham • Assistant Dean Scharron Clayton • Dr. Norris Durham • Dr. Martin Edwards • Dr. Jon Hall • Dr. Noel Harold Kaylor, Jr. • Dr. Barbara Lounsberry • Dr. Charles Means • Dr. Karen Mitchell • Dr. Mary Rohrberger • Dr. Dale Ross • Dr. Paul J. Siddens • Dr. Donald Shepardson • Dr. Kay Stensrud • Dr. David Walker • Dr. David Whitsett • Nancy Bramhall • Becky Burns • Greg Clark • Judy Cole • Barb Davis • Ed Ebert • Bernard Edelman • Mary Huber • Osie Johnson • Judi Kikendall • Kris Knebel • Steve McCrea • Michelle Parrini • Ruth Ratliff • Sara Salisbury • Sue Stilwell • Todd Studebaker • Sharman Thuren • Lynda Van Devanter • Amy RohrBerg Wilson • Janet Witt • Kadija Timbo • The casts and crews of IOWA STORIES and VIETNAMESE CHESS • Our families • Pages 13 and 43 of VC • And the students in 00:192, Exploratory Seminar—Vietnam: Perspectives and Performance.

Table of Contents

FOREWORD.. vii
ACKNOWLEDGEMENTS.................................. viii
INTRODUCTION... 1
IOWA STORIES: THE VIETNAM EXPERIENCE
    Introduction... 7
    Iowa Stories... 11
VIETNAMESE CHESS
    Introduction... 80
    Vietnamese Chess...................................... 89
AFTERWORD... 163
ABOUT THE AUTHORS 165

Introduction

> "There is no one out there to whom I can communicate what I saw and what I thought and how I felt."
> —*Vietnamese Chess*

> "I just had to realize they didn't know the true story behind it all...."
> —*Iowa Stories: The Vietnam Experience*

Veterans' personal stories of their experiences during and after the Vietnam War are accounts uniquely revealing of the difficulties, the challenges, the horrors, the injustices, and the coping struggles men and women carry as a part of their lives. Some stories are difficult to tell, but may be damaging to the teller if kept untold. Some stories contain the potential to create understanding and to document important information; these stories are a resource for communities to become more aware of the details and complexities of events such as the Vietnam War, and to share in the work of analyzing their impact and response.

The scripts in this volume, which are works featuring the veterans' stories, result from ethnographic research and oral history interviewing, and both scripts have been performed as interpreters theatre productions. The construction of each script is a combination of creative writing, editing and arranging of interview excerpts, and interweaving other texts of Vietnam: letters, poems, diaries, and songs. Both performance projects featured the presentation of the veterans' personal narratives; in the course of creating productions, the researchers/writers were immersed in months of informal interaction and formal, tape-recorded interviewing. The transformation of these stories to another performance genre requires application of the information, empathy, and insight the writers gain from intensive interviewing augmented by observation/participation in veterans' support groups and social events.

As scripts developed into performances, as part of the University of Northern Iowa Interpreters Theatre program, cast members also became researchers, talking with veterans to develop understandings of the war and the roles they were to play. The first production, IOWA STORIES: THE VIETNAM EXPERIENCE, toured high schools and colleges and performed at the Vietnam War Memorial in Washington, DC. The second project, VIETNAMESE CHESS, was performed on-campus for audiences of college students, veterans, and community members. It was partially funded by the Iowa Humanities Board. Both productions, according to the conventions of interpreters theatre, involved the audience by addressing personal stories directly to them as well as to characters within the dramatic scene, and by the use of metaphoric sets and action (instead of completely literalized scenery and movement).

Oral history's potential to increase and deepen one's understanding of events such as war becomes clear in these scripts, even in the partial experiences made available in this volume to the reader. The veterans' own voices speak, and are augmented by conjoining their narratives. The power of the personal narrative is enhanced by this performance style's mixture of actual and imagined action, scenery, costuming, and props. VIETNAMESE CHESS used a metaphoric life-size chessboard as central stage area; the IOWA STORIES stage contained actual military props, a camouflage backdrop, and uniforms to create the sense of the Vietnam settings. Traditionally a genre of performance based in

Introduction

triggering audience imagination and participation, contemporary group performance of texts combines aural and visual cues, ranging from extensive to sparse, to create or suggest physical location, mood, and time. Interpreters theatre productions stage single works of fiction and non-fiction; or they employ scripts combining texts, either weaving together such texts as court documents, short stories, essays, news reports, poems, music, and folktales, or presenting the multiple texts implied within one work (a short story with its embedded rituals, celebrations, myths, oral history, or gossip, for example). Group performance scripts traditionally retain and feature narrative forms and use the staging methods which result, rather than reworking narrative into dialogue. Relationships between past and present selves, between storyteller attitude and character experience, or between conversation and story are featured in the script structure and in the staging approaches.

The powerful and engaging voices of actual people in oral history texts are even further enhanced by the embodiment of them in performance. Editing of oral history texts essentially condenses or omits, for the demands of the performance, event time; such editing and arranging of narrative and other directing choices involve further phases of understanding and interpretation. The insights regarding the veterans' experiences transform as they are translated into casting choices, movement concepts, and other production decisions. As ethnographers who also script and direct performances, the creators of the scripts in this volume share their research as it has evolved in the collaborative efforts and continual investigation that comprises a production process.

Current research in personal narrative and oral history proposes that the stories we tell of our lives make sense of what happens to us and serve to inform, persuade, or explain to others our desired interpretations. The audiences of these oral history interviews consist of the envisioned audiences of a production in addition to the interviewers who originally elicited and taped them. Research data is a combination of the interests and focus of the interviewer, the envisioned productions, and other potential publications of the texts, and the veterans' views, experiences, and purposes in the telling. Oral history in performance reenacts history, reinterprets it, repeats it, and retells it. Cast members relive the veterans' personal experiences and create the presence of experience with an audience; the narrative text is an individual recollection that tells and interprets from specific and collective points of view. The perspectives of the scriptors/adaptors, the performers, and the directors further retell and reinterpret both the individual stories and the cultural story of the Vietnam War and the Iowa soldiers. The works presented in this volume join other current investigations of the complex and significant processes of collecting and performing oral history narrative.

PHYLLIS SCOTT CARLIN
PROFESSOR OF COMMUNICATION & PERFORMANCE STUDIES
OCTOBER 1993

For further investigation:

Carlin, Phyllis Scott. "From Ethnography to Social Action through Oral History in Performance." Presented to the Speech Communication Association, November 15, 1986. ERIC ED 293 174.

———. "'That Black Fall': Farm Crisis Narratives." In *Performance, Culture, and Identity*. Elizabeth C. Fine and Jean Haskell Speer, eds. Praeger, 1992, pp. 135-156.

Pollock, Della. "Telling the Told: Performing *Like a Family*." *Oral History Review* 18 (Fall 1990), p. 1-36.

IOWA STORIES: THE VIETNAM EXPERIENCE
by
Marilyn Shaw

Iowa Stories: The Vietnam Experience

Introduction

"What do you know about Vietnam?" This question seemed simple enough, but what I discovered after asking it to my teenage daughter and several groups of high school and college students in the spring of 1989 was troublesome. For some time I had wondered myself about this era of history. I had vague recollections concerning the Vietnam Conflict. If my knowledge of this era was so sketchy, what knowledge of it did those students sitting in my classroom possess? Not only did I find that their knowledge was sparse, but that no one seemed willing to discuss Vietnam with them or help them find answers to their concerns. From this beginning, IOWA STORIES became a reality.

In researching this period in our history, I found that there were legal documents, facts, and figures available, but I wanted more. I didn't want the story reported by news media and information released to the public by the government, but the story of those men and women who were actually there. With this question in mind, the next ten months of my life became interwoven with the lives of the men and women of Iowa who were willing to invite me into their past and share their personal recollections of Vietnam. From these interviews, IOWA STORIES was conceived.

The mission of IOWA STORIES was to assist the public in gaining a more in-depth knowledge and a better understanding of the contributions that Iowans made during the Vietnam Conflict. While this mission was achieved, it is apparent today that IOWA STORIES did much more than just educate. Four years later I am still receiving inquiries concerning the show and still visiting with Vietnam veterans about their experiences. Through sharing their personal experiences, IOWA STORIES provided catharsis for them.

IOWA STORIES belongs to the Vietnam veterans of Iowa and to any other Vietnam veteran who can find a glimpse of him or herself within the text. Many veterans shared with me that this was "their story," whether I had interviewed them or not. During the first run of IOWA STORIES, many vets would return night after night, bringing family members or friends. After our opening performance, one of the vets interviewed requested that his brothers and sisters attend the next evening's performance. He wanted them to attend without him and to call him afterward. Upon leaving the theatre that evening, one of his sisters came up to me crying and stated, "I wish I had known what it was like for him before. I'm so grateful that I know the story now. Now we are going to go find [him] and tell him how proud we are of him and how much we love him." With new understanding and compassion, this family came together after twenty years.

After collecting and transcribing personal accounts, the stories were compiled into a script discussing the veterans' decisions for entering military service, their adapting to the change and accepting what was happening in their lives, and their struggle for survival. Although it was my intention at the beginning to produce four of five performances on campus and at local schools, IOWA STORIES proved to be in great demand. For the next ten months the cast and crew engaged in a vigorous schedule of performances throughout Iowa and into our neighboring states. Our performance beside the Vietnam Veterans Memorial Wall in July, 1990, was one of the high points of the tour. With the support of the veterans across Iowa, their families, the University of Northern Iowa, and the office of Senator Charles E. Grassley, IOWA STORIES journeyed to Washington, DC, to share with the country the story of those Iowans who gave of themselves during this conflict. We were not just a cast and crew making this journey, but representatives of Iowa's Vietnam veterans. This was one of the highest honors these men and women bestowed upon us.

IOWA STORIES is intended to provide an overview of a time when our young men and women—youthful and in top-notch condition—were used as weapons by society. This is not a story about one or two Iowans, but about all Vietnam veterans who shared similar experiences. In scripting these stories, I chose to interweave the stories of multiple individuals into the text because the stories appeared to have universal qualities. While there are nine performers, more than twenty-seven veterans are represented. Using this intertextual approach, makes it apparent that these experiences possess a universal theme. The stories collected share common threads tied together by this universal theme. There was no attempt to take a political stand or to come to a resolution on the merits or failings of this conflict. IOWA STORIES is a compilation of stories of men and women who were ordinary people called upon to do an extraordinary job. As one of the vets said, "You can hate the war, but don't hate the warrior, because the warrior is just doing what he [or she] was trained to do."

NOTES ON STAGING

The set for this production is very presentational. Because of the narrative structure and the oral history element that is crucial to this production, only a few stage directions or suggestions are appropriate. The composition of the cast is essential in bringing to life these stories. Therefore, each director and each cast needs to create its own vision and work that angle to create unity and design.

MARILYN SHAW
OCTOBER 1993

Vietnam: Perspectives and Performance

IOWA STORIES:
THE VIETNAM EXPERIENCE

Originally performed February 22 and February 24-5, 1990, at the University of Northern Iowa, Cedar Falls, Iowa.

ORIGINAL CAST

Sam Graeve	Myra Cody	David Turner
Mark Giesler	Teresa Shaw	Mat Krull
Chris Ellsbury	Jennifer Terry	Jason Menke

Compiled and Directed by Marilyn Shaw

Set Design..Kirk Shaw
Light Design......................................Paul J. Siddens III
Vocal Accompanist...................................Michele Shaw
Coordinator of Interpretation......................Phyllis Carlin

1990 TOUR OF DUTY

February 22, 24, 25	UNI, Cedar Falls, IA
March 4	UNI, Cedar Falls, IA
March 6	West Waterloo High, Waterloo, IA
March 27	Maquoketa Valley High, Delhi, IA
March 30	Central Methodist College, Fayette, MO
April 5	Cedar Falls High, Cedar Falls, IA
April 9	Belle Plaine, IA
April 17	Waverly-Shell Rock High, Waverly, IA
April 18	Kirkwood Comm. College, Cedar Rapids, IA
April 19	Brooklyn, IA
April 22	Marshalltown Comm. College, Marshalltown, IA
April 25	Mount Mercy College, Cedar Rapids, IA
April 26	Hudson Schools, Hudson, IA
April 30	SAC's on Seventh, Waterloo, IA
June 24	Vietnam Veterans Memorial, Des Moines, IA
July 3	Vietnam Veterans Memorial, Washington, DC
August 4	Herbert Hoover Auditorium, West Branch, IA
August 10	Iowa Central Comm. College, Fort Dodge, IA
September 23	Vietnam Vets Memorial Vigil, Waterloo, IA
November 3	SCA National Convention, Chicago, IL
November 8	Closure Performance, UNI, Cedar Falls, IA

Iowa Stories: The Vietnam Experience

PROLOGUE

Music fades in on the dark stage. Any song that produces a feeling of remembrance and reflection into the past is appropriate. As the song fades, a light comes up behind the scrim. The performers are lined up one behind the other to recite the opening poem. As they complete their lines, they move off alternately, the first to the left, the second to the right, and so on. This is done in a very mechanical and orderly style.

DAVE. Walk with me, my son,
 To hear my stories of lost battles,
 Of a war that could not be won.
MARK. I'll talk to you of men
 Who left their homes,
 Pride in their hearts,
 Muscles of stone.
SAM. Proud warriors of our country,
 Ready and trained to fight.
 Soldiers that now cry of nightmares,
 Night by night.
JASON. Listen to my words of damaged
 And body-scarred men,
 Crippled minds that cannot mend.
CHRIS. No marching band's or
 Hero's welcome came to be.
 We're forgotten soldiers,
 Remembered only by me.
MATHEW. For we are not those glorious warriors
 That you read of, my son,
 Only forgotten soldiers of a war
 That could not be won.

UPSTAGE

A=Ammo crates
B=Block (1.5' x 1.5' x 1.5')
F=Footlocker
H=Halfblock (1.5' x 1.5' x 0.75')
L=L-Block (3' x 3' x 1.5')
S=Sandbags (4)   T=Tire

DOWNSTAGE

Sandbags are on the upstage side of a 4x4 platform stage-right, and an old jeep tire rests against it downstage. A footlocker sits on the upstage side of a 4x4 platform at stage-left, and ammo crates lean against it, one downstage and another upstage-left. The L-shaped block is placed upstage center-right, square blocks are seen center-left and in front of the tire at stage right, and a halfblock is downstage of the stage-left platform.

Full lights. Performers enter and take various places on stage. There is a feeling of distance among the members throughout the scene.

Iowa Stories: The Vietnam Experience

PART ONE

OF THE LAND

DAVE. I was—I volunteered for the service when I was—two months after I turned seventeen; and then I went through my basic training and my AIT training and went to Germany. Just after my eighteenth birthday, I went to Vietnam.

MATHEW. I got out of high school and I had a chance to go to college on a music scholarship. I didn't really want to go. I didn't really want to do anything. That's... (*laughs*)...I was glad to be out of school; I don't know. Back then, they—the draft was really heavy. I was drafted in '65 and that's when they built up and you really couldn't—unless you really had your goals set to go to college and accomplish something or whatever, you didn't have any other choice. You either had to have your whole life planned out, or you were draft bait. That was it, unless you had an exemption of some sort.

MYRA. My father sort of raised me on wartime stories from WW II, and it was very clear to me that the best part of his life was in the Army. He loved it. And I couldn't afford college. I wanted to get a Bachelor's degree in Nursing. I had been working as a nurse's aide since I was sixteen and I always wanted to be a nurse. It was very congruent with my family's value system that you make a contribution to society. My family was very supportive of my being a nurse, but we couldn't afford anything. I was reading literature and it was clear even then to the counselor that I needed a Bachelor's degree and I couldn't afford that. I had researched and knew the Army would pay my way, so I got into the Army as soon as I could so I could go to college.

Vietnam: Perspectives and Performance

SAM. My country afforded me the opportunity to get an education. I had no doubt about the sincerity of the people that I came in contact with, my elders and the people at college who assisted me to go through school. When it came time—when I wanted to go on to graduate school, I was not accepted because my draft board changed my classification to 1-A. So I enlisted, just beating the induction papers. It really wasn't a choice. I was knowing that I had to fulfill the obligation when Uncle Sam called. And it's so amazing—the same day I shipped away on my regular enlistment, my induction papers were in the mail room—the very same morning.

CHRIS. After I registered for the draft, they sent me my induction notice. Then, just for giggles, I went down and took my induction physical and I flunked it because I had a history of knee trouble. So I didn't—I forget what my rating was; something like 4- .... Whatever the rating is they give you for "available for recall at a later date."

I wasn't a good student. I wanted to party. (*Laughs.*) I certainly wasn't a good student. I flunked out of Wartburg and then enrolled in Marshalltown Community College on probation, and that was in the fall of '65. Then I got my grades up that first semester so I stayed. I wasn't on probation the second semester, so I goofed off again and I had to hurry up and get myself back into summer school before I'd get drafted that summer. That was '66. I finished at Marshalltown the first of February, 1967. I wasn't going to enroll because I knew I wasn't paying attention in college; I was wasting my money. There's no sense of me even staying, so I just—I knew I was going to get drafted and I kept putting it off and putting it off. Well, I was anticipating when I was going to get my draft notice and it didn't come and didn't come....

-14-

Iowa Stories: The Vietnam Experience

So, rather than go through the anxiety, in March I went down and volunteered for it. Thirteen days later they sent me my induction papers. I just went in and volunteered. I said, you know, "Just draft me! You might as well take me as soon as some other poor sucker. Just take me a week earlier."

JENNIFER. I was planning to teach school, all right. I had a teaching degree and I was looking through *National Education Teaching Journal* and there was an ad in there for Special Services and it had this picture of this woman in a total blue uniform standing in front of the Eiffel Tower, under the caption, "You'll never be the same." (*Laughs.*) And I thought, "You know, going to Europe sounds like much more fun than teaching in Iowa." (*Laughs.*)

So, I applied and I went through the interview process and the FBI and the CIA and everything else was checking up on me, and I was supposed to go to Germany. I was scheduled to go to Germany, and about a month before I left I got this phone call from Washington and they said, "Well, um, we're overstaffed in Germany right now, but we have some openings in other parts of the world. How about if we send you to Vietnam instead?" (*Laughs.*) At which point I went into hysterics.

Well, that didn't sound like such a good idea to me, but I thought, "Let's see...does this mean that I won't get to go anywhere?" So, I didn't bother to ask. I was kind of in shock. So I just said, "Yeah, okay." And that was where I got sent, and I never regretted it. You know, if I had the choice now, that's where I would choose, but at the time....

My brother was in the Navy already and my parents were petrified that he was going to have to go to

– 15 –

Vietnam: Perspectives and Performance

Vietnam, and he ended up in dry dock in San Francisco. And I had to tell them that their daughter was going. That wasn't a real popular evening.

DAVE. I didn't really know what Vietnam was. I just knew I wanted to get into the Air Force. I wanted to go into the service, and I didn't have any long-range goals, so to say. I just wanted to get away, go to the service, get that out of the way and then get back to school.

MARK. I was in college—in junior college. I wanted to stay out and work for a while, but I knew they'd draft me, so I just walked into the draft one day. First I went to take a physical, see if I could pass. I passed it. I walked in and said, "I'm here to volunteer."

They said, "As soon as you sign this paper, you're gone."

And I said, "That's okay." I wanted my name moved to the top of the list, but I didn't anticipate ending up in the infantry, because I had two years of college. I thought I'd get a desk job or something. But then, February of 1967, things were just starting to heat up then. I went into the Army in January and ended up in Vietnam in July.

TERESA. I felt that it was my duty to go and I did volunteer to go. I was career by that point in time and I felt it was my job to go. It was no more right for me to go than for a man to go. I was in the Army.

JASON. I went a semester to school and started second semester. My draft number was 110 and they were at 108, so five of us decided. I was only taking 13 hours; and to stay in school, or to get back second semester and to stay out, you had to take 15 hours and go to summer school. Well, I didn't decide to go to summer school and there was five of us and we got together and decided to all go in at the same time. So after a week, we quit

−16−

Iowa Stories: The Vietnam Experience

Ellsworth and we all got together and went in together.

DAVE. I went to the Air Force because my father was in the Air Force. By joining the Air Force, I advanced in Specialty areas—well, commandos. I went back to Vietnam as an Air/Sea Rescue.

JENNIFER. I graduated in the spring but I went back to participate in some theatre while I was waiting to go over there. Most of my friends thought I was going to Germany. It was strange. I had been in a...peace march—it wasn't a peace march. It was a protest on campus for—I don't even remember what. And, I knew I was going to Vietnam and I was thinking, "You're marching in this thing and you don't even know what it's about?" And so maybe the peace marches were starting and everything, and I thought maybe I ought to find out what that's all about. I thought it might be a good idea.

MATHEW. Nineteen sixty-five. I had two friends that graduated ahead of me. They were both in the Marines, they both were discharged from the Marine Corps, and both of them had been in Vietnam. And I asked them where they had been in there. I was interested in the Marine Corps, you know. I was curious. I asked them if they had to go to Vietnam and they both said, "Yes," and that's all they said. They just looked at me and said, "You don't want to go there. It's just a place you don't want to go. Stay in college." I didn't listen to them very well. (*Laughs.*)

TERESA. I was very young when WW II was on, but I just happened to see a copy of *Life* magazine and on the cover was a woman who at that time was flying aircraft from factory to factory and flying missions for the aircraft, dragging these balloons that the other planes took target practice on, things like this. I said at that

– 17 –

time, "When I grow up, that's what I'm going to do." I guess I never forgot about that.

JASON.   You know, just being an American. Just a sense of patriotic duty.

Iowa Stories: The Vietnam Experience

UPSTAGE

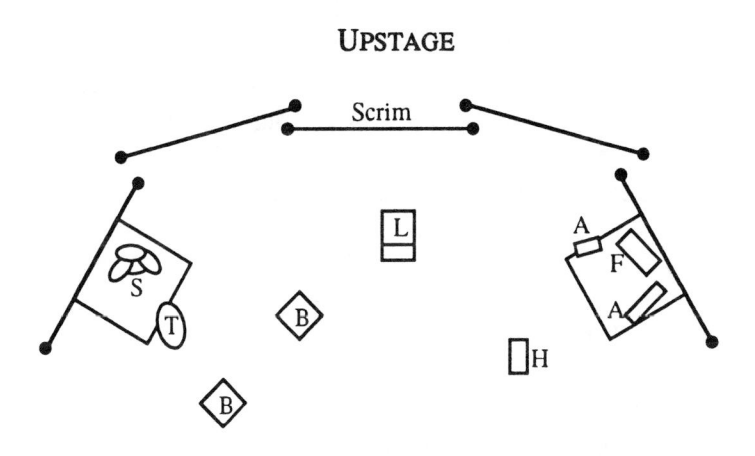

DOWNSTAGE

Halflight. The L-shaped block is moved upstage center. The square block upstage center-left is moved beside the square downstage right. DAVE enters and assumes position downstage center. He now is enacting the role of the drill sergeant. The rest of the cast form a straight line facing the audience. Lights come up full and the squad is taken through a drill. They march single file, circling the stage. (Several different cadences could be used. Select one which is comfortable for the cast and suitable for the audience.) As the cadence draws to a close, the entire cast exits stage left. As the marching ceases and the lights fade to black ,we hear only the drill sergeant and the sound of footsteps coming to a definite halt.

Vietnam: Perspectives and Performance

TEMPERING THE EDGE

MARK.   I didn't really mind basic training. There were guys that—I mean, they hated every second of it. It was preparatory. It taught you the military code of justice; it taught you what you can do and can't do. It got you physical. It showed to your best ability that you could do it. It did have its points. I mean you got yelled at, but that's just part of it—to see what you could do, what they could get you to do.

SAM.   I'm cynical. You know, I expected to go into basic training to be in preparation, but one of the problems of the trainers was: theirs was a personal experience that they'd experienced; and they in no way can prepare all of the basic trainees coming through a basic training program to be prepared for every contingency, from the branch of artillery, to the grunt, to the chopper pilot. The training basically gets you to shape up physically and act when you're given an order by someone in command. When there is no longer somebody in command and you're faced with responsibilities for somebody else, you're not prepared.

MYRA.   It was a lot of routine stuff: how to wear a uniform; a little bit of marching stuff; the paper work, because the paper work we did in the Army hospitals was a little different. It's like going in training for a different hospital, sort of an orientation period. We also learned to do tracheotomies, debridements, and sutures.

TERESA.   I've always been a questioning person, and I ran into a lot of problems because, I mean, some of the things you were told to do just didn't make sense to me, and I wanted to know why. You know, "Explain this; that's not the way it is." I mean, they're looking for reaction. "You do what we say and without questioning." And I built sidewalks because I asked, "Why?" I had to paint buildings. I had to wash insides of buildings because I asked, "Why?" One time I caught a girl who fainted in formation, and that's when I ended up cleaning the barracks, an empty barracks. We ended up cleaning the barracks, the girl who fainted and me.

CHRIS. The whole idea of basic training, or any training that you took, was to survive, you know. They weren't interested in your personal opinion or your physical ability or anything. If you could do what they told you to do, then you qualified. Their idea is to tear you down and then mold you into any way they want you to be. They did a good job of that.

MARK. We'd get up about six o'clock in the morning, go eat breakfast, train for a little bit, run out to the ranges. Everything was geared to shooting—to me it was. We did a lot of running. We ran thirty miles a day: ten out, ten back.... We had diseases going around all the time. Our soldiers were dying. We had a couple of guys in our company die because they would run and just get exhausted. Spinal meningitis, we had two guys die of that. Well, then they cut back and trucked us everywhere. We had a couple of drill sergeants. Once they got out, they...they made you get off the truck and run the rest of the way, you know. It was—you'd go until nine, ten o'clock at night.

MATHEW. Well, you were degraded to such a level that you had very little self-respect, self-esteem for yourself. The military built you and, I would say, brainwashed you into a fighting machine that you—your training was to kill, and that was your mission, without thinking.

SAM. We were young people, and you take people 21 years down to 18 years, and you take an adult human being the way we were raised, to respect—our generation was raised to respect our fathers and adult people, you know, in our lives. So you get this adult screaming in your ear every single day, 18 hours a day. We're talking rough, rough days. You got them screaming in your ear to kill or be killed; calling you names like *maggot, lowlife, scumbag,* everything they feel can make you feel—belittle you in order to make you this fighting machine. I don't care if you're a Rhodes scholar or Einstein, you're going to react. Human nature is to survive. That's it. Once you do, you become what they want you to be. You either do or you won't make it.

DAVE.   I didn't think it was that bad, not nearly as bad as I thought it would be. I went to Fort Polk, Louisiana. They called it "Little Vietnam." We flew right in as a unit. Everything was painted black and yellow—black and yellow stripes because this was TIGERLAND and you were becoming tigers. Everywhere we went we had to growl like a tiger.

Scrim light comes on, silhouetting a soldier doing push-ups.

If you got out of step, you'd have to drop and do 20 pushups and growl like a tiger, or run around the telephone pole 30 or 40 times and growl like a tiger the whole time. Standing in the mess hall, everything was five foot apart. We were conditioning ourselves not to group and bunch up. We'd be in line at parade rest and the drill sergeant would say, "GIVE ME FIVE TIGERS!"

Soldier jumps up and gives five growls. Scrim light snaps off.

JASON.   After I was done there and I landed in Vietnam, I can see and honestly say we should have never slept in a bed. They should have piled a 100-pound rucksack on us and, yeah, it would have been tougher, but it would have been better for us.

CHRIS. You spend your whole time wondering why these officers and why these NCOs are so serious all the time. I spent all my time in basic thinking: "Someday I'm going to like this guy." I'm talking sergeants and my lieutenant—I hated their guts. That's a natural reaction, but I always thought in the back of my head, "This is going to end someday." But then you get to a real war and you realize why they were so serious. They're trying to save your ass.

JENNIFER. The nearer I got to going—it really didn't hit me until I knew I was going. And then, of course, you get the jitters. I mean, if you didn't, you wouldn't be human.

JASON. It's kind of a bittersweet thought. I guess you do and you don't. You want to experience it and you don't. You can't vision yourself getting hit. Then, on the other hand, you don't know what it feels like to be hurt like that. Maybe it doesn't hurt. It's got to—even in the movies people scream!

MARK. My mother was really upset. She was not happy at all. She...she couldn't say, "Gee, you can't go." She wouldn't—would never be the one to say, "Oh, this is a dumb thing," or, "I don't want you to go." It just wasn't the thing to do. She had a brother that was in the Phillipines, you know, during the Second World War, and he ended up in a mental institution for the rest of his life. So that had a real effect on her. And she didn't want me to go, but she had to...just grin and bear it.

SAM. I understand my family to have been angered. I had to put things on hold—my struggle coming from a kind of lower-income family and going through college and wanting to have the opportunity to go on to graduate school being interrupted by the military service. But everything was just, "Wait a minute. Time out. You can't do what you want to do. You're going to do what is asked of you." That's why it's sort of unfair, when we look back on the service time.

CHRIS. I was in the Army. I was in Fort Lewis, Washington. Nobody knew until I came home. I had, something like...two weeks, I think. I just showed up at home one day. My mother: "What are you doing home?"

"Because I've got something to tell you." And I told her and it was bad. She was upset. Father had no reaction. He was a WW II veteran in the Navy, so he really didn't know what I was up against. I didn't either. He didn't—his war experience was going to be totally different than mine was. He didn't relate to the Army.

DAVE. My mother, this is typical of my mother, though, because she doesn't accept my alcoholism, and when I was going to Vietnam it was more—not that she didn't love me—but it was more like, "Oh, he's going to be all right." I don't think she wants to face the reality itself, so it's easier to ignore. Most of my friends wanted to know, "Why in the hell do you want to go over there?"

"That's where it's happening."

MATHEW. There were several kids in my area, Tama, Toledo—the school district—that had been killed. I think it was five. So, you know, it hit Mom real hard. It was my turn to go, just—she didn't understand why. She didn't balk. "Well, it's your duty. You enlisted, you've been picked. I guess you've got to go." Yet she was real apprehensive. I don't know how I'd react if one of my kids had to go. I just don't know. They sure better have the POWs home before they do go.

JASON picks up a block, moves downstage left, then sits on it. As he speaks, the others form a farewell line, with CHRIS playing the part of the soldier.

JASON.   I've got a large family and lots of friends. When I went out to the airport, my whole family stood in line and several friends of mine and...it was, you know...I went right down the line and gave them all kisses and everything and each one of them was crying for the feeling that they would never see me again, 'cause—as I went down the line I tried not to show tears either, but as soon as I kissed my mom and dad, it...it hurt. And yet I tried to tell them that I had good luck and everything else, so don't even worry about anything. I'd probably just, you know, be way back, in the back someplace. I tried to say anything, I could not have them worry.

CHRIS sits on the block downstage right as the other cast members except JASON exit.

But as soon as I turned my back and headed for the airplane, I just...inside...kind of like it blew up, but I wouldn't dare turn around or nothing. I just had a... heavy feeling. "Is this the last time I would see them all?" And it hurt.

Vietnam: Perspectives and Performance

UPSTAGE

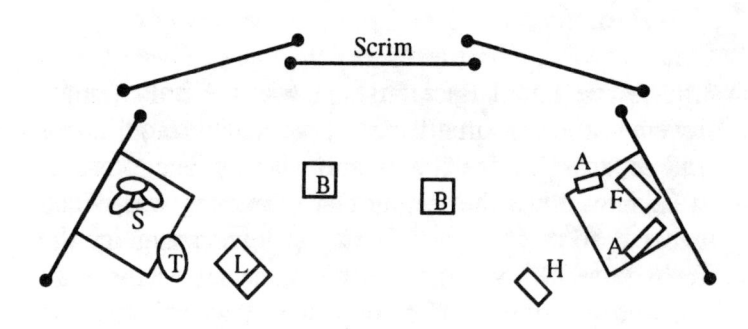

DOWNSTAGE

Lights out. L-shaped block is moved downstage center-right. A square block is placed upstage center-right and the other center-left. The halfblock is downstage left. Lights come up 1/4. Music begins softly, and slowly becomes louder, but not full. The song is, "I'm Leaving on a Jet Plane," performed by Britt Small and Festival.* On the line,"I'll wear your ring," JENNIFER enters stage left and moves to downstage center. As she begins speaking, music fades completely and lights come up full. Cast appears more cohesive in this scene.

---

* Music used with permission from Britt Small and Festival. Contact the Association for Textual Study and Production for more information.

Iowa Stories: The Vietnam Experience

APPROACHING THE EDGE

JENNIFER. I was the only female on the plane. I had to go to Travis Air Force Base first. I was the only female assigned there at that time. I walked through and I looked down to see if my shirt was buttoned, 'cause, you know, I had the feeling that something was wrong because all these eyes were just following me. It was really unnerving. And on the plane I was the only woman and...it was a Pan Am flight.

Okay. And we flew in to Tan Son Nhut. People were pretty quiet, not a lot of talking, not a lot of visiting. It was...it was a bit tense. Everybody looked a little frightened at that point. A lot of culture shock. I saw a lot of very alien things to me, very quickly. I got off the plane. I went into the terminal...I didn't know where to go, I just followed the guys. I just followed the crowd. I went into the terminal and I stood in line and this guy at the desk said, "Oh, women don't have to stand in line. You just come up here to the desk and we'll take care of you right away." And the guys didn't mind a bit; of course, they weren't in any hurry to get there. (*Laughs.*)

So, yeah, they just took me right up there and through the processing, you know—checked my papers, no big deal. And then they had a...Special Services had a jeep waiting there for me to take me down to the office. It was no problem. And then, the next days I had to go through...well, it was almost the next week, really...all kinds of processing. All over Saigon. I remember at the office they took me in this little room and they gave me this whole pile of stuff to read, all these brochures and everything, you know. And I thought, "Well, okay."

So I started going through them, started reading, and all of a sudden this little red warning light goes off, because the semester before I had just taken Discussion and Debate and I thought, "I'm reading American propaganda here!" (*Laughs.*) "This is really ridiculous." And so the rest of the time I read it, I was picking out the faulty arguments, you know, and everything. (*Laughs.*) I was feeling very superior that I had that knowledge, you know.

TERESA. We flew commercial, contracted by the government...I think it was International Airlines...I can't remember anymore. Brightly colored plane...which was, of course, maximum capacity...filled. I was the only female on the flight. We stopped in Hawaii for a short break and I was met there by a WAC from the Pacific. That was a surprise to me...come out of the plane and welcomes me. She had another officer with her who had served in Vietnam, and while waiting for the plane to refuel and everything we went inside and had a cocktail, and then it was time to go and I got back on the plane, and it was awfully hot...I just remember that... even when we were airborne, it was humid, hot...the air conditioning wasn't sufficient. Crowded. I mean, just packed in there like sardines.

DAVE. We stopped at...let's see...from Oakland we went to Anchorage, Alaska, and we got off while they refueled, and it was colder than hell there. (*Laughs.*) We were in our khaki uniforms, short sleeves. From there we went to Wake Island and Okinawa. Wake Island was just a little dinky island. The aircraft came in and the nose was over the water when we stopped. They had to pull us back until we turned around, and when we took off, the wheels touched the water. I didn't know if we'd make it to Vietnam. Then we stopped in Okinawa and then into Cam Ranh Bay. The flight took about 17 hours.

MATHEW. I know how cattle feel when they get slaughtered. Thirty-two hundred guys on a ship that was made to hold about 1600. It was called the USS Gordon, it was a merchant marine, and we were packed in there like sardines. We went through a typhoon off the coast of Formosa. Threw us around like a cork in the sea and everybody got sick and I was...I was happy.

"You know, it's funny," I thought. At one time I drove all the way to Des Moines to join the Navy, that was my original contact with the military, and they refused me because I'm color-blind. I went home and I got drafted, and I went on this ship and I thought—after about six days of being seasick—I thought, "Boy, this could have been my career."

I was so glad when we got there. It was mixed emotions. We landed, and on the shore they were firing artillery fire and we could see gun ships along the way and all this noise—explosions. And I was thinking, "Well...." You had such mixed feelings. It was like, "If I go on land, there's a chance they may blow me up. If I stay on this ship, I'm going to be sick." There's not much to choose from; there really isn't.

TERESA. Everyone was quiet; everyone was dead serious. I think we were really meditating on what to prepare for. And very little communication, everybody was very, very quiet, and nobody seemed very...friendly. I mean, we would ask somebody for a cigarette light but...with that serious venture, I think we were preparing for it. Not to become tied...bond between each other.

Cast freezes. The scrim light comes on and MARK's silhouette is seen. He delivers this speech from behind the scrim.

Vietnam: Perspectives and Performance

MARK. The beginning of an end. Sadness in leaving, apprehension, loneliness. If only in a word, "Goodbye," could one see the return of a loved one or a friend.

MYRA. We left from Travis Air Force Base and we went through Alaska. The main thing that I remember about the trip was we got off the plane in Alaska for a break and we were talking in the lounge trying to get to know each other—nobody knew one another. We were just chattering and some civilians at a table behind us were making some extremely rude remarks which they would never dream of making to total strangers under different circumstances. But because for some reason—because we were in uniform and on a plane to Vietnam—we were fair game. And I...I experienced that several times during that time period. They seemed to think it was okay to make extremely rude remarks to people in uniform that they had never seen before in their entire life. A lot of anger about the political issue was taken out directly on the military personnel. It was very obvious to me that we were fair game and that it was okay. If you chose to put on a uniform you were supposed to expect that people were going to react in public. It was basically anti-social behavior that society was condoning.

SAM. You had no idea, no concept. There is no way to tell anybody what war is all about. I mean, it is ridiculous. I sit here every week, at least once every week, and I hear comments such as, "Well, Vietnam. Those things happen." "Everybody's got to do their duty." And these comments are always from people who were never involved in it.

TERESA. Adaptability—so very important in this existence.

CHRIS. My first impression was that it was about a thousand years behind time, because the people never

had soap or they just, you know, wore the same clothes all the time. Like, the little kids just wore a little shirt, they never wore anything below their belt. Then the older people, they'd wear the same clothes maybe about six months, six or eight months, the same set of clothes all the time. And their houses would be wide open, and you could go in there and they'd be asleep, like sleeping outside. And when I got there, it was real hot....
TERESA. It's nothing you imagined like it would be.
A connection with one another is now beginning to become very noticeable.
CHRIS. It's almost surrealistic. It's almost like...like you're in a time warp, you know. You can't believe this could possibly happen to living human beings, somebody that you know. And then the taste and the smell....
DAVE. It smelled like I was in a garbage dump. That was my first impression of it. To me, it's strange. And then our convoy—not our convoy...our escort—got sniped on the way to the replacement center, so right away we.... (*Chuckles.*)
JASON. Yeah. The first thing you look for is the bunkers, because they tell you at no certain time, you know, they can drop mortars or rockets any time of the day. So you prepare for and try to find...you're always trying to find an exit or the nearest bunker, the first place to dive for.
SAM. It's a gorgeous country. If Holiday Inn and Ramada Inn could ever sign a deal with those people they'd have it made because it's the most beautiful piece of land I've ever been on. The mountains and everything...it's gorgeous, gorgeous. You know, that...that back there is my most vivid memory and I can still see it today. Then you start looking down and you see the slime and the death and all that.

Vietnam: Perspectives and Performance

MATHEW. Of course, the minute you walked off the plane you wanted a gun. They took us right through, middle of the afternoon...never will forget...right through the middle of Pleiku. People everywhere. We had no guns or anything. Then we went to the base camp. Divisional Base is a big place! I don't know how many soldiers. Man, they're the support for everything. Never will forget, we got just to the edge and we had to dismount because everything was mud...trucks couldn't move in it. The road ended at the end of the village.

TERESA. I remember the heat and...just the first week it was just mainly getting oriented and finding out what my duties were going to be and responsibilities and meeting, of course, the new people. It went by very rapidly, the first week.

MARK. I was so scared. And, you know, it's the fear of the unknown. You didn't know what to expect. It wasn't anything like I expected it to be because I was in the mountains. What we saw on TV was all down south in the jungles and swamps.

JASON. It felt like 120° and it would be that hot and raining. It didn't matter that you didn't wear your rain gear, 'cause as soon as you were in the sunlight you'd just sweat!

DAVE. The humidity was real bad. You talk to somebody who was in the jungle all the time and ask them and that's what they will tell you. It was real bad because there you've got to watch the jungle itself along with the war. And it always rained on you. I remember going through this swamp place and it rained leeches. It made you become an animal. At night we made a hooch, and we took the three ponchos and made a little lean-to. There were some cold nights because we were in the mountains. I remember one night there was a monsoon that just tore everything down in sight. Those monsoons, they'd rain all night and all day, just like you had a bucket of water dumped on you. Then the sun would come out, and those jungle fatigues would dry right now. (*Snaps fingers.*) Then you would wait 20 minutes and it would rain again.

TERESA. We arrived early in the morning and, of course, the minute you walk out the door it hits you and you feel like you're drenched immediately. And they were hustling everybody around and we had to run from the plane into the reception area because they were still—this was still during Tet of '68, and so it was just hurry up, hurry up—and really, I think for everybody, nobody really knew what was going on. I mean it was just... you'd do this and you'd do that....

MYRA. It was like this humongous germ hanging over your head waiting to get you. It was hot, humid, and dirty.

JENNIFER. We really felt out of place. We were called "Newbies," and the term fit.

MYRA. We landed in Bien Hoa, which was ten miles from Long Binh...where the 90th Replacement people... where everybody in Processed was. And I remember we got herded onto these big buses, and they were fire-bombing buses at the time and I knew that. They herded us onto these big buses and then MPs lined up between the buses and in front of the buses and behind the buses with their machine guns mounted on the jeeps...you know, one guy driving the jeep and one guy standing by the machine gun...and I knew we were in trouble.

MARK. When we came in to Cam Ranh, I think we were processed in like...two days. We went from Cam Ranh Bay to Da Nang to Quang Tri where we trucked up to Dong Ha and that was like the third day I was in-country...third day, maybe fourth day at the most. The first night at Dong Ha we took incoming rockets. I thought, "Dear Lord?" So I was already wondering what I had gotten myself into.

SAM.　　We got there around 11:15, and it was good and hot. And they...they were trying to get us off the plane before the rockets blew us up. Noticed a line of body-bags lying there. You got tough real quick once you were there.

A lot of people didn't even look; they just kept going, and you'd be passing—as you're going off, troops would be going home...and the look on their faces was like, you know, you didn't know what you were getting into. Some of these guys had a dead stare, and they were just out of it. They were going home.

A lot of the guys going home would be throwing comments to the rear. They'd be calling, "You fucking new guys," and stuff like that, you know. "Welcome to Vietnam. I'm glad I'm leaving." It was a real strange thing when you got there. All the guys going home and you'd be coming in. You'd look at them and they'd just shake their heads. You kind of thought, "What's going on? What are we getting into?"

TERESA.　　Well...the rookie element is still there. It never stops. If you become comfortable with the idea of knowing that you're in a hostile element...I don't think I had. I didn't live with that fear that I initially had when I was first in-country. I became more relaxed about that. You just didn't think about it as much. I mean, you had too much other to think about. I hated the night. I hated the night with a passion. I longed for the daylight every day I was there.

Iowa Stories: The Vietnam Experience

UPSTAGE

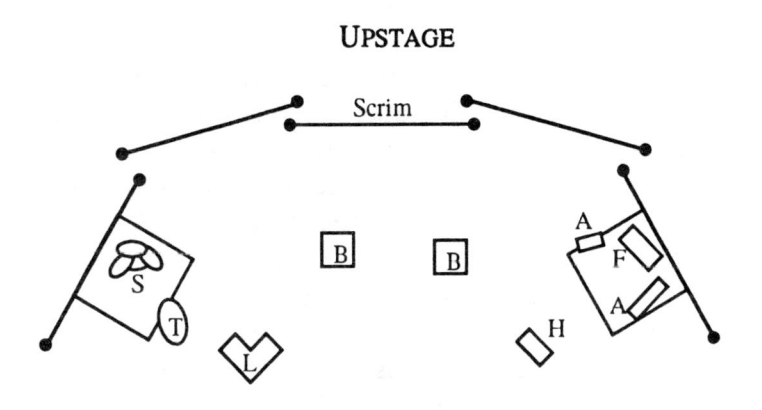

Scrim

DOWNSTAGE

Lights down. Everyone exits the stage. Downstage right is an L-shaped block lying on its side. The sound of helicopters begins low and rises to high intensity. Music then begins to fade in, slow and frightening. CHRIS *enters stage right, moves toward center, then sits on center block. Lights come up to about 1/3, just enough to see his face and reactions. He moves stage right to begin his monologue.*

ON THE EDGE

CHRIS. The first day we got there we got hit by rockets, the very first day. But after the first blast of rocket attacks it was kind of quiet. Actually, it was kind of quiet up until Tet of '68—the Tet Offensive—and then things started getting lively around there.

Slowly he eases up and moves to the L-block and it becomes the bunker he remembers.

We had close to 2000 Vietnamese try to storm the Air Force base overnight. I was...about three other guys... me and two other guys got stuck in a bunker for over twelve hours. Rusty...

Lights come on behind scrim. The scene is enacted as CHRIS remembers.

...that's a story. He got hit in the chest and I was holding a sucking-chest-wound in the guy for twelve hours...and he died...with me and the others in the bunker. He just passed away eventually...but we were holding off the Vietnamese, the VC attacked us. The Army and the Air Force couldn't get to us 'cause we were the most extended bunker in the base. They had over-run our bunker three times. They had to drop ammunition to us twice.

I think if we could have gotten him out of there earlier he'd still be alive today, but we were trapped. They couldn't get to us. It was a situation like, you're out there 150...200 yards outside from the base perimeter and they're around us, trying to get into this bunker. Dropping bombs, killing everybody around. They're trying to come in, we're trying to keep them out. There's not much you can do, you know? Bullets are flying, there's gun smoke everywhere and the gooks are coming at you through the door, through the window; and it's hot....

Rusty stayed alive as long as he could. We didn't have any plasma. I was going direct. My commander kinda chewed me out for it, but he said, "You did what you had to do and, damn it, you did what you were trained." There were guys in the same bunker that had the same blood types. I had a tube and I was going direct. I was pumping direct even from my own arm. I was keeping blood in him, you know, but he got to the point where he was so weak....

Rusty was conscious for about 12 of those hours. He...he knew what was going on, and I knew what was going on. I told him, "I can't do anything. All I can do is keep you from bleeding to death."

He told me, he says, "I know, but you've got to survive. You've got to get out of this. You go back and tell my family what happened." He made me promise, and I did.

Scrim snaps off.

Right there was probably the hardest thing in the world to do—go see his family and tell them I was there, that I was trying to save him and he died. You know, they forgave me, but...it was drilled into our heads, never leave a comrade down. You do everything you can, but it was drilled into our heads that you never leave anybody behind. And I just—you know, for years I had a real problem with failure. A lot of it was because of that.

CHRIS slumps down in his bunker as JENNIFER enters.

JENNIFER. I don't remember very often being afraid in Vietnam. It was really strange. It's like...you live with that every day so you just...sort of accepted it, you know. You didn't really think about it all the time, even when the rockets were coming in. Anyway, if it's got my name on it, it's got my name on it, you know? It was like an old John Wayne movie, like being in the wagon train, just...enclosed. Secluded. But also it really brought us all together. The camaraderie and the...the responsibility for each other was incredible. It was like we were cut off from the rest of the world. Just...that was a world of our own.

JASON. One time, we were sitting on the outside of the trail, waiting, and I had this thing in my head saying, "This is your last day, man." I just knew it was going to be our last day. So, I did everything I could to—I had my men all in position exactly like I wanted them to keep an eye on what we were looking for. We had the traps and everything set up in a special way. I just kept saying, "This is it. Somehow they are going to get more that just a couple of guys; they're going to come in and...this is going to be it for me."

I was very well armed. I had an M-16. I also had a shot, grenades, everything I needed. I had all my—I also had a .38 pistol with me just laid out. Just perfect. And I still didn't feel I had enough. I mean, everything was just set up for—I could take on a whole platoon by myself. That's the way I had everything set up. I tried to tell myself that it..."I'm not going to get killed today...." But still I just...I knew it was my last day.

I felt this way for hours and one of my guys in my squad came over and started talking to me. It was a complete whisper. Somehow he got me out of it. He got me into...to believe that it wasn't going to be my day, that I had made it through hours, and now I just felt it was going to be it.

MATHEW. I had a really good friend from Hawaii that was a

squad leader, and we went out on this mission, a search-and-destroy mission. We were out all day and a lot of people got wounded, and I found out one guy got killed, and that was the guy I had bunked with back in Hawaii. We were in the same room, and we were only there maybe a couple of weeks, and that was really sad because we were just like brothers. I was just sure that he was going to make it, and I thought he was a better leader than me, but out of the whole outfit there was only one guy killed, and that was him. And that kind of shocked me because that was my best friend in the outfit, and that happened right away, and I was really sad.

Oh, I couldn't talk to anybody about it. A lot of people were talking about it. I really remember that better than anything. I think that was the hardest part of Vietnam, that people you knew...you might know them, but then maybe five minutes later they might be dead. They were quite young.

CHRIS rises and exits stage right.

TERESA. In my off-hours I was just so exhausted. All I wanted to do was sleep, if possible. In the nighttime I found that extremely difficult because we were so close to the perimeter that you'd hear everything from the machine guns going off; you'd hear the flares popping at night, and of course that makes you wonder, "Is Charlie coming in?" And all the guys awake out there in the bunker line...so to me, sleeping was difficult.

MATHEW. We had a tunnel compound nearby, and we could hear 'em digging at night, and then—in fact, we put up radar to see any movement, if they moved above ground, but we never did detect them too much. They generally moved in the early evening before it got dark. But... kind of a mystery, a lot of it. Like, they'd have ox carts and oxen going down the road and everything, or bicycles. Well, it'd just give you an indication you're gonna get more in the dead of night.

MARK. Along the Cambodia-Vietnam border they had—for lack of a better term—these cadre would have "pow-wows." You know, they'd get together and a commander from this unit would come and a commander from that unit and they'd coordinate their military strategy. Who's doing what, who's where.

So when the commanders got together we tried to sort out the intelligence to find out where they met...or if one was going to be in the village. In order to do this, we had a series of spies, generally young girls ages 13 to 16 somewhere, who would get into these villages by, you know, there's a relative there or there's...blood connection somehow: cousin, uncle, aunt, grandfather, someone—her sister had married a guy from that tribe. I mean, they...somehow they got there. They were already in place by the time I got there.

I mean, there's a lot more to it than that, but the story in a nut shell, that's how we did it. We'd go in...we'd set up a perimeter around the village and wait until...until our chance to nab them and then we'd grab them, interrogate them, and then kill them.

Lights come up behind scrim. One figure is sneaking up on the other to enact MARK's description.

They also had a perimeter set up, too, and you'd have to work your way through them to get in. So there was a lot of...silent killing. Grab them by the throat like so, and cut their head off. That's how it worked.

Scrim snaps off.

Spooky. It scares me to...to know I got to do that. The 'gnards did most of it, but when you had to, you did it. You did it. It needed to be done. It was going to

Iowa Stories: The Vietnam Experience

help us win the war. It took me a while to talk myself into doing it. But, like they say, once you get that taste of blood, it's...it's a fix. (*Pause.*) And it's real hard to come to...to come to terms with it. It wasn't then.

TERESA. At first, I was fascinated riding in helicopters, looking out into the jungle...until the first time we were fired upon. I guess it had escaped me why this is dangerous: down below us is the enemy. But, I mean, puffs of black smoke hit and I didn't even...I still didn't realize. I mean, the machine gunner was sitting behind me and tapped me on the head and said, "That's Charlie." At that time the helicopter just peeled over, and he started taking evasive moves. If I hadn't been strapped in, I would have gone right out the door. I remember that so well, and I remember from that time on I wasn't so free to hang out the side of the helicopter as I had been.

SAM. I worked in an orphanage. I would go out to an orphanage and to a leper colony...really got to know people that way. This leprosy was not the contagious type. These people, they had some of the biggest pigs you ever seen in your life. They had huge, huge pigs. They just loved it when we came out because we carried rice and mash. The nuns ran it, and the one nun who ran it kept telling me she was VC. "I VC. I not Vietnam. I VC." She left North Vietnam because of her religion, so she decided to be a nun in a leper colony. She was just...always joking. She was a neat lady.

MYRA. I can remember driving to a medcap one time.... Our preventive medicine officer was a pediatrician, so he organized the nurses on their days off to go out to the orphanages to provide medical help to the orphans. Anyway, we went to insecure areas, and I remember... well, we left one orphanage right ahead of a firefight one day. We could hear them coming when we left. We were in an off-limits area, too, because we went to places where the kids were. We got through it okay. I really don't know how we pulled that one off. We just did it and took off. Evidently we were just small time and they weren't after us. We got down to an area where the orphanage was, and it was okay, and we went home by a different route.

JENNIFER. It was Christmas Eve, and the Thais had invited me over to their camp for a party that night, okay. So it's Christmas Eve and I'm going over to that party with a bunch of Buddhists. (*Laughs.*) And I was feeling kind of depressed: "Oh, I don't know if I'm doing the right thing or anything."

They took me in a jeep across camp, and it was a beautiful night...there was a big moon...and we were going across camp and I looked up on this hill and here were these snowmen up there. And I thought, "No, I'm seeing things," you know. (*Laughs.*) So I said, "Wait. Stop the jeep. Drive up there." I just couldn't believe this.

And it turned out some of the guys had taken sandbags, and painted them white, and set up this whole snowman family up on top of this hill—you know, little hats and everything on them—clothing and stuff, you know. It was military stuff, but I just couldn't believe it. That was wonderful.

I'll never forget that image of looking up there and seeing those snowmen on top of that hill. It was so incongruous. It wasn't anything I expected to see, and it changed my whole mood from that moment, you know. I found depression to just...be totally relieved. I know it sounds like a silly thing, but most things that affected you...shoot, were very simple.

Iowa Stories: The Vietnam Experience

DAVE. Christmas of '67. We were close to Cambodia. We were about three miles away. The Vietnamese had carried some 105 artillery up this nearby mountain... piece by piece! They were shelling our fire base with it, and it took two days to get permission to knock it out. It took ten minutes to knock it out and silence it. And I know what happened. It was during the Christmas truce, and it had to have gone all the way back to Westmoreland for sure. Maybe it went farther than that to get the okay to, "Okay, knock that gun out."
Cast freezes as scrim light comes up. CHRIS's silhouette is seen.
CHRIS. Will we all want to get up and leave when it's over? Or will we sit back and wait for the second showing to start before we realize it is the same poor performance as the first? The players become weary, but the audience brings them back with applause and cheers. Little do they know the majority of the act was ad-lib, and the royalties are not paid. The actors, like puppets, cannot reason, and are unable to move without the control of the master puppeteer.
Scrim light out.
TERESA. It was exciting...never a dull moment...being rocketed almost every night. For a while...for starters... it was every night, several times a night. After a while, like everything else, you said, "Oh, here it comes again." "The *mamasans* went home early, that must mean the base is going to get rocketed." (*Laughs.*) That was a good sign. The Vietnamese disappeared. We knew something was up.
SAM. We got hit pretty hard. We had quite an artillery barrage, and it lasted about three days. That's...that's probably about the most memorable moment other than...I brought a guy home from Cambodia. A dead

– 43 –

man. He was coming home, I brought him home. I was—at the time I thought I was responsible for his death since I—it was one of those times I froze on the machine gun, and I thought they needed the machine gun real, real bad. I didn't fire it for...oh, I bet, 30 seconds. It's just that I froze. I finally...came to my senses...he was already dead. (*Pause.*) It's just—I always wondered whether or not it was my fault. But, we were quite deep...well, not deep...
Scrim light comes on; the following is enacted.
...we were twenty miles into Cambodia. They wanted to leave him there and I said, "No." It was going to take us three days to get back to Vietnam to get him out. So, I knew I was going to have to carry him. They left me alone—me and two other Montagnard fellows, they helped me out a bit. They carried—by the time I got him to Vietnam he was in pretty bad shape. He was falling apart. But his body came home, you know. I always thank myself for doing that. At least his mother got to have him again. But it was a bad deal.
Scrim light snaps off.

JENNIFER. We could never depend on anything. More people were out in the field, more units. They would stay out for longer periods of time. Sometimes the service club would be absolutely empty. There would be just nobody there. We would just close it down and just wander around and talk to the guys who were around. Our programming, you know, we just forgot that. I'd just pull something out whenever somebody was there.

The way the troops reacted was very different, too. They changed. They'd come back into the club, and they'd always tell us what was going on, you know, out in the field, and what had happened and so forth. After Tet, they got quiet. They weren't as exuberant; they'd stand around in the rain, and we'd walk by, and they'd just stare. I don't know, they all looked shell-shocked. There was a very different mood.

TERESA. From daylight to long after dark...it was nothing but work. I never worked less than 14 to 16 hours a day, and that was every day of the week. It was tiring, it was physically draining, emotionally draining. I was in-country ten days exactly when we were first rocketed. So that was always a constant threat. You never knew when they were going to come in, so you always had that fear in the back of your mind. I recall the absolute terror that I experienced when we were rocketed for that first time. It took me a good thirty minutes to calm down after it was all over with. I was shaking so badly...it scared me that badly. I think that really hit me...that really brought it all home, you know.

JASON. We took re-supply within a six-day period, so we carried rations for feeding ourselves. Everything was on our back. Our helmets were on our back. We operated sweeping through areas, and when we needed to have a supply bird, we'd sweep through areas to clear a place to put down our re-supplies. Bring in the mail... about a 21-day run. We would go for refitting and to get our hair cut. Spit-and-polish and refurbish losses we had suffered in equipment—radios—and some days it would be one-day-in and right-back-out to another area.

MARK. Well, I carried eight canteens and was always out of water. We got re-supplied every three days. Nine meals. They'd send us water from the rear, and they'd send it in 105 artillery round shells filled with water. Take 'em by chopper and drop 'em out to us. We got a change of clothes once a month, whether we needed it or not. We got a sack of pants, a sack of shirts, sacks of socks...we didn't wear any underwear. And we just go grab one, and if it didn't fit you, just switch with your buddy. But it just didn't matter, because ten minutes later you were filthy again. You'd become such an animal...you'd go sit down in the mud and take a break.

MATHEW. We had one site I really didn't like to go to at all. It was on top of a mountain...we called it the Hill...Hill 78, or something like that. We had a radio relay up there, and the only way in and out was by helicopter. The VC owned the bottom of the mountain, we owned the top of the hill. I always had that fear of having to spend the night up there, and I never wanted that to happen. I had a deep fear of that. We had to...they did have protection, of course, a company of Infantry up there that patrolled and...of course, it was well fortified, but just the idea they could creep up that mountain at night and attack...I always was happy once we lifted off from that place and returned. Looking out for me, I guess.

JENNIFER. I was majoring in Speech and Theatre, okay, with an English minor. Well, I went over thinking I was going to be directing plays and entertainment, you know. When I got sent to Phouc Vinh—which was just a brigade, a field camp—Tet broke out, and so there was no way I could even think of directing a play. I mean, to cast a play and then have your cast go out into the field and not come back again...you never knew from day to day. You could never depend on anything.

DAVE. The first six months I was over there it was hit-and-miss, hit-and-miss. We really wanted to find them. They played a game with us. From the Tet Offensive on, they came out of the trees in uniform and regiments, and it was more like it should be. We didn't have any problem tackling them, just as long as we could find them.

CHRIS. They operated in groups, where they had little groups of three men here, three men there, three men here, then they'd have a rendezvous point. So, rendezvous and hit us, then split up into those little groups again. Well, you can look for just three men and never find them. They harassed us, but that's what jungle warfare is, I guess. But we didn't have any problem killing them, just finding them.

For a long time, as I marched through the jungle there, I couldn't figure out why we never saw any other Americans or found out were they had been or what they had seen. The news said we had 900,000 men. Well, that's a lot of people. But, when you start thinking about it, it takes nine men in the rear to support one man in the field, so we only had about 100,000 in the field; the rest were back in the rear.

DAVE. I was feeling better as I went on. At first, I was kind of down, 'cause I knew I had a long way to go, and I knew a lot of people were getting killed, and you always figured it was just a number of days before it was your turn. And I mean, we had quite a turnover, you know, a percentage of people getting wounded or killed, and death was coming pretty often and pretty fast every day. You always had to think about the enemy 24 hours a day, and I think what happened to a lot of young soldiers...they never realized that at first. When they first landed, you know, they just knew that death was close, and they were careless a little bit, where when you got close to the end of your tour, you took more care of yourself, 'cause you were thinking, "If I make it a few days more, I'm gonna get home." And that's what everybody did, and everybody was just miserable and wondering when they could get out of Vietnam, 'cause it was a bad experience.

Vietnam: Perspectives and Performance

MYRA. Unweariness to a person, I think. Keeps them on edge. I mean, it...because you never knew...you never knew. Following your—even though you'd been in-country—I mean, there's always that element of not knowing. And you never knew where they were going to hit or what was going to happen. That never left you. At least, it never left me.

JASON. When I first got over there—I'd say about the third or fourth week I was there—we went out to the bunker line one night to check to make sure they had enough water and stuff like that. Heard one of the bunkers say that one of the guys went back to the john and didn't come back yet. They said he had been gone about 15 minutes. Well, that was long, but we didn't quite think about it right off the bat.

So we went on cruising down the line and called back and he had been gone 25 minutes. We decided that maybe we should go back...and the outhouses sat back on the other side of the road. We stopped and started to walk up to it and we heard a thump. We thought that was kind of strange, but we didn't think of it. We were getting hit with mortar. One of us flew the door open, and this kid had an M-79 and pulled the trigger. Off the trigger was a "Dear John" letter.

That was real tragic, my first experience with death. Suicide to me is awful hard. I don't know why; to me it is a waste. Why would a woman write a guy that went to the service, you know, over to Vietnam, a "Dear John" letter? That was hard to understand.

Sound of helicopters slowly rises.

I s'pose...over the year I seen...about twenty go like that. There was just an awful lot of it.

Lights fade out with the sound of helicopters.

END PART ONE

Iowa Stories: The Vietnam Experience

UPSTAGE

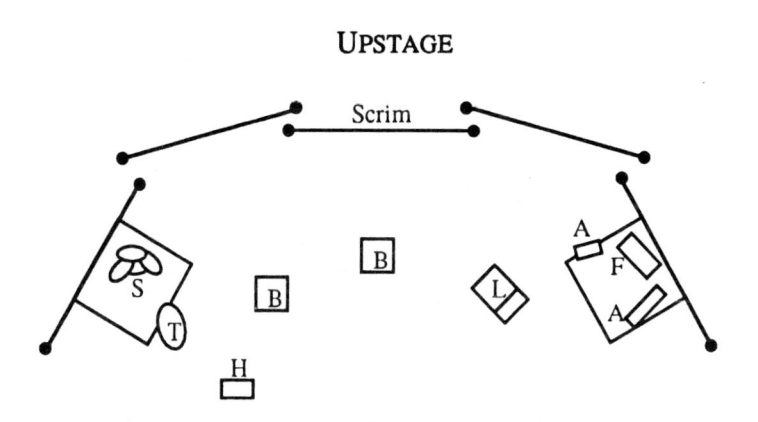

DOWNSTAGE

Full lights. L-block has been moved stage-left center. A square block is placed upstage center and the two remaining blocks are stage right—one in front of the tire and the other slightly downstage and to the right of it.

PART TWO

LETTERS

MARK. We got mail almost every chance—every night, just before sunset, I would make sure my squad was always perfectly shaped and everything and then I would get back and take off everything except for, you know, my clothes. Sit down in the bush, start thinking. I'd try to write a letter to my wife...we were engaged then. So, I'd try to write a little bit. I'd lie quite a bit. I'd tell her that we were way in the background. We hadn't seen anything.

DAVE. I didn't want to write home and tell my mom, "Oh, I killed three gooks today. Wasn't too bad." What else are you going to tell them?
"What did you do?"
"Oh, I went down to the club, got drunk." Make it a party all the time? I really didn't want to tell them, so I started making up stuff.

CHRIS. It's just, "Hi, Mom. I love you." Never told her that before. "I'm counting the days. I'll be home in March. See ya later." I guess...kind of...casual.

SAM. I did discuss it because I was in a combat area, and I was married and had kids, and I wanted them to know what was going on. And so, I discussed it with them, and it was a big build-up that they knew what was happening, and they'd tell you about it.

MATHEW. I'd talk about my dog or about the USO show that was in town. Or I went to Saigon. Went out and had a few drinks and saw a movie. I went to the zoo. You know, stuff. You didn't want to tell them about going out on missions, that kind of stuff. I'd mention it once in a while. "We had a rough mission the other day." I'd

Iowa Stories: The Vietnam Experience

leave it there. I didn't want to get in-depth. I didn't really want my mom to know.

JENNIFER. Actually, I did pretty much talk with my parents about it, because...we're a very close family and, like I said, they have always been very supportive of everything. Once I was there, and there wasn't anything they could do about it, they didn't begrudge me that or anything...just quite the opposite. And my grandparents were the same way. They wrote constantly. I even got—my grandfather never wrote a letter—he wrote me a letter, you know.

I got this letter from them. They had seen a television broadcast about some action that was going on around Phouc Vinh, and the broadcast apparently made it sound like the whole camp was just wiped out. Decimated. And they were just frantic, so when they got my letter and found out that I was alive and that everything was okay, they wrote back and told me what had happened—that night it was supposed to have happened I was at a party at the Officers Club, okay. So I thought, you know, it's going to be better for me to let them know where things are. I said, "If anything really happens, I'll let you know. So don't listen to the news media," or whatever. We heard so many false reports about things that were happening.

MYRA. I discussed work only in how many hours that we had put in. As to what was going on around us, or in the field of battle, I did not. Number one, I felt they didn't care. That was the impression I got, and that's what you kept hearing, you know, all the anti-Vietnam sentiment back stateside.

TERESA. In August of 1968, I didn't receive one piece of mail for the entire month, and I was devastated. Each day—I mean, everybody...they hawked the mail. They

-51-

knew exactly when it was due in—it was just so important. But I didn't hear from anybody for the entire month. And I just...I think I felt a little sorry for myself, as a matter of fact, you know—they didn't care. I mean, didn't they know what was going on over here? Weren't they concerned? I remember even to this day because it grew as the days went by with no mail. I was almost embarrassed to go ask the mail clerk, "Did I have any mail?" because, "I'm sorry, Ma'am. No mail today. Maybe tomorrow." That went on for a month, and I was really down...really down.

DAVE. There was an old saying that was used very often in Vietnam. The guy that told me the saying said, "It don't mean nothing...shit happens." A very, very used saying. That's the way you got to look at it. It don't mean nothing...shit happens. Keep on going. If you let it bother you, it'll waste you. Sooner or later you make mistakes. It's best to put it back in your head, put it away, and get on going; and that's the way a lot of guys got back to the States. You keep putting it back; you put it far enough back and pretty soon it comes back out. You've got to deal with everything.

JASON. I was just thinking, you know, what I had to do...if I wanted to live, to come home...because a year is a long time in this area, and it was very difficult to cope with, and you had this—you always had to watch yourself. You never knew when they were going to attack or what was going to happen. You were just counting the days when you'd go home. Almost everybody kept a calendar, how many days they had to go, and that worried them constantly. They kept up with it every day.

MATHEW. The shorter you got, the better you felt. It was kind of a boost, because like, the first six months you had so long to go, you figured you were never going to get out of Vietnam. Then when you were getting short, you were feeling better; your morale picked up.

TERESA. The shorter you get, the more nervous you get, because you feel, "I've made it this far and nothing happened." Within a month of the time that I was to leave...we were rocketed this one night and it hit just behind my hooch, and an officer that I knew was—he had only seven days left in-country and was going to meet his wife in Hawaii—and he was killed. And it just—you think how close that was to you again and you escaped it. We couldn't fire back because it came from "a friendly village." So we had to take it, but we couldn't do anything in retaliation.

CHRIS. It was a great feeling knowing that I was going home. They decided that if you had over ten months in-country or been wounded or something, or you had ten months and you were out-of-country, it wouldn't do any good to send you back for about a month, so they would rotate you back. And I was pretty close to ten months, and this kind of worried me because you feel that one of these times, you're not going to get wounded...you're going to get killed.

JENNIFER. I was in a fog by that time. I don't know if it was alcoholic fog or fever or both. But I just...I was sort of...I don't know. It was like it wasn't quite real. I was moving mechanically. Going through the motions. They finally sent a couple of new girls I was supposed to train and stuff. During my last month, they had three units in there, just moving them in and out. They couldn't decide if they wanted to put anyone there...I don't know. Troop movement was something else at that time—very unsettled all of a sudden, where before, you know...I was so busy, just keeping...just transferring inventory from one unit to another because we had to get permission for the new units. It was a lot of paperwork...lot of business, and it just was like it had already ended for me and I was just going through the motions. Emotionally it was the same way, you know, I...I wasn't close to anybody anymore. I was just sort of there on my own. Just a hanger-on, you know, and the new girls coming in were very anxious to see me go so they could start their own programs.

Scrim light comes on; MYRA is in silhouette.

MYRA.   Returning home. Almost like starting school in the fall. To see old friends and family again. Everyone had changed, but in ways I'm not familiar with yet. The joy of a reunion scene so sweet, yet still half a world to go.

Iowa Stories: The Vietnam Experience

UPSTAGE

DOWNSTAGE

Lights up 1/2. Music: "Still in Saigon," by Britt Small and Festival. Fades when performers are in place. L-shaped block moves upstage center, onr square blocks is downstage right in front of tire; and the other block is stage left off the corner of the platform.

LEAVING THE EDGE

MARK. We were about 36,000 feet in the air... (*chuckles*)...'cause everybody was afraid they were going to shoot us down. You take off over the jungle and...you aren't free yet, you aren't clear yet—not until you are out of their space. So I never felt totally safe until we were cruising.

CHRIS. I got home early. I hadn't planned on coming right home. I kind of wanted to be a civilian for a couple of days, but then I decided, "Well, no. Let's just go home. My mother wants to see me." I just...out of the blue, you know...I got to Cedar Rapids, Iowa, and I called her. I said, "You're not going to believe this, Mom, but I'm in Cedar Rapids." And these people—this was my first confrontation with society. They wouldn't even rent me a car. You know, I had a lot of money sitting in front of her, and she wouldn't let me drive a car to Toledo, Iowa. I said, "Give me a break!"

I needed a credit card. Hell, I didn't even know what they were! I need a credit card, I need a letter of reference, and I was a GI and they wouldn't rent cars to GIs. And I'm going, "Well, thank you very much." Boy, if I ever was going to hit a broad, that's when I was going to do her, right there. I said, "No, she's not—it's not her policy. I'll just shut up and call my mother." So you know that frustrated me, real bad. By this time the airport is closing, and the janitors are there, and I'm going to be sitting out in this March storm. I didn't want to call her. I just...I was at wits end. I should have taken a cab and gone to a motel.

SAM. There was a group of us that were together coming back. We ran into a big executive from Phillips

Iowa Stories: The Vietnam Experience

Petroleum, and he wanted to know if we were coming from Vietnam and a couple of the guys didn't want to say anything, and I said, "Well, yeah," still in kind of a daze or whatever.

And he says, "Can I buy you a drink?"

And I said, "Yeah, I could really use one."

So I started drinking, and we had like four hours til the airplane, so he took us up to the executive suite at the airport and paid for all the drinks, and we were getting smashed. I was anyway. I was about three sheets in the wind when I got on the airplane.

Well, one guy sitting across or next to us, whatever...we were having a gay old time and they were... just out of the blue he said, "You guys from Vietnam? Just back from Vietnam?"

I said, "Yeah."

"Oh, a bunch of baby-killers."

Of course, I just freaked out. I almost killed the guy. Then the police came in and walked me off to jail. The guy from Phillips Petroleum, he just couldn't believe what happened. Some of the guys I was flying with knew about Ben...[I had tried to adopt him and he was killed 3 days before I left]...and they told the story, and the Petroleum fella from New York had the company lawyer come out and try to get me out. They treated me decently; it wasn't like I was a criminal or anything. They had heard the things that the other guy was telling me that made it happen, and they were understanding. I think they knew I wasn't really like that...just an instantaneous reaction that I couldn't help.

DAVE.   I remember coming home. My girlfriend and my family met me at Rock Island at the bus depot. I get off the bus and I go up there and say, "Hi," to my family, you know. My Mom's hugging me and my girlfriend's hugging me and my dad's shaking my hand and I don't feel anything. You know, I felt absolutely nothing. No emotion, no anything. Nothing like, "Hey, I'm home." You know, you see the old movie where the sailor gets off the ship and he hugs his girl. That famous poster, everybody's seen it. Nothing. Nothing like that.

TERESA. I was a little frightened. Happy. I was happy to come back, and yet Vietnam had become the known, and I was coming back to a world which was the unknown for me. Also knowing all the sentiment back stateside... I wondered how I would react to that and what I'd do if someone spit on me because I know I wouldn't be responsible for my reaction. It didn't happen to me, thank God, although it did happen to many—eggs thrown at them. I came in late at night and in the wee hours of the morning in San Francisco. I was quick to catch a flight to Seattle. I went from one terminal in San Francisco, the military terminal, to the other one by bus. I had very little contact that way. I never wore my uniform again until I reported into my assignment.

JASON. The only welcome I got when I got home—my mother knew I was getting short. The night I came home, I surprised her at the restaurant she was working at. She didn't know I was coming home then, and I walked in on her while she was in the dining room of the restaurant, and we hugged and cried for a while, but that was it. My homecoming was my mother in the restaurant. There was no....

MATHEW. I got hit with some dog shit outside San Francisco the second time I came back. Baggies with dog crap. I got called a baby-killer right here in Cedar Falls, Iowa, by a very good friend of mine. Still friends today. They didn't understand what a person was going through over there...they had no concept. If they did, they wouldn't have done that. I was so very young. They didn't understand what the GI was going through...the emotions of being away from home... probably the first time for a lot of Vietnam guys...in a very strange and stressful situation, and then coming back to the world and getting treated like dirt.

I just had to realize they didn't know the true story behind it all and that's why I am so adamant about education. These people may never change, but I am expecting maybe a better attitude toward those who went. I just want them to accept the fact that you can hate the war, but don't hate the warrior, because the warrior is just doing what he was trained to do. The warrior doesn't like the war to begin with. That's why he's a warrior...to stop the war. You can't hate the warrior.

There were 150,000 Iowa people who went over to fight a war and, by golly, they ought to think about that. These guys who were Vietnam vets, they went over to do a job, and they should get a little respect. They don't need a lot, just a little respect would go a long ways. Just a, "Glad you're home," would go a long ways. You'll see a lot of us vets welcoming each other home.

TERESA. I resent the fact that the sentiment that existed stateside...that I allowed myself to feel guilty. It was a sense of guilt, like who's right and who's wrong. I tried to forget that I'd been there. I never wore my ribbons at duty. The only time I would put on my ribbons was at a command function. I just didn't want anybody to know...I didn't want to talk about it. I just didn't.

MARK. It was kind of a shocking experience, nobody seemed to care. It was a new world, nobody seemed to care. Nobody knew you were a Vietnam veteran, nobody paid any attention to you, except when I got on the plane. I was in uniform, and they made an announcement on the plane that they had a Vietnam veteran on board going to Chicago, and I was on standby, and they found out I was a Vietnam veteran and they made sure I got home as fast as possible on the plane. This airline company took good care of you, because when I got to San Francisco, I thought I'd have to wait a long time for an airplane, but they said, "No, if you run down that ramp, you can get one in 5 minutes," and I was excited.

JENNIFER. For me it was not a problem, because I had a friend living in San Francisco who went to college in Theatre, and he had invited me to stay in San Francisco with him for a few days when I got back. So as soon as I landed there...he lived in this residence hotel and I had a room with a sink and running water. I thought it was wonderful. (*Laughs.*) He sort of seemed to sense that I needed time, and he said, "When you want to do something, let me know and we'll do it together, or if you want to do it alone, that's fine." So I had that for about a week before I even went home.

Then when I went home to my family, they had flowers. My dad wrote a poem and everything for me. And it was Christmas time then, and I went out to buy a tree and this guy wouldn't let me pay for the tree when he found out I was a Vietnam veteran. I had a very different homecoming from what the guys describe. So you know that was—then we also at that time had— some of the Service Club personnel and some of the guys who had been at Phouc Vinh made arrangements that a bunch of us were going to meet in the DC area for New Year's. I went to DC, but I got snowbound at O'Hare Airport in Chicago. Missed the reunion.

When I got to DC—and I loved it. There was no

snow, so I moved there. People that I knew were constantly there, in and out, and they always stayed at my apartment and everything...people from Phouc Vinh. I still had that contact for quite some time, so I was able to gradually....

SAM. I got spat on out here at the airport. When we landed, there was a guy from Oelwein who was in the Marines that came back with me. When we got off the airplane, we were stone-assed drunk. I figured I was going to be an alcoholic the rest of my life 'cause I was drinking pretty heavy. And the stewardess woke us up. We noticed all this foam out there. Well, they had foamed the runways because one of the landing gears didn't come down. I thought, "Hey, here I've been in Vietnam and didn't get a scratch, but landed here and almost died and I was passed out." Just kind of a rude awakening.

We went into the terminal and he had his Marine uniform on and I had my Army uniform on, and we got spat at by a couple of kids. I was kind of furious about it, you know. They spit on my medals. I don't appreciate that at all. I told them. The Marine guy just kind of held me back. He says, "Just ignore them." So we each went on our own way.

I was out there for about a half an hour waiting for my wife, so I finally called her. They came out...it must have been about 5 minutes because they only lived down the road from the airport. We went back to the house for a couple of hours, and we had reservations at the Ramada Inn, one of the suites there. About 8:00 we left...got there and the Shriners were having a big thing there.

This guy said, "Hey, you just come back from Vietnam?"

I said, "Yeah."

"Hey, we'll pick up the tab for you. You guys eaten yet?"

"No."

"We'll take you over here to the restaurant."

I said, "Well, we'll get something after a bit, once we get settled here."

He rode the elevator with us and we went up to the ninth floor, and he walked us to our room and told me to carry the bride across the threshold. I said, "Okay."

He said, "Is there anything I can get you?"

I said, "No, this is where it stops. We'll meet you down there later for dinner." This was just the opposite—getting spit on, and these guys were just the opposite, you know. They didn't prod questions or anything. We just talked.

JENNIFER. When I left DC, I went to California—Los Angeles. I was writing then, and I was going to write about Vietnam, and I went to a Seminar at UCLA. One of the big publishers from New York was there talking to our class, and the first thing he said was, "If any of you are writing about Vietnam, don't send it to me. We don't want it." So I thought, "Well, there went that." That sort of ended that for me for quite a few years. "Nobody wants to hear about it."

TERESA. I've talked to so few people about Vietnam because I just don't talk about it easily. I still feel, you know, I spent my year over there and certainly it took its physical and emotional toll, but I came back all in one piece. I'm whole, as far as anybody can tell, but emotionally it takes a toll. I mean, physically as well, and it bothered me for...it still bothers me. It still bothers me.

Scrim lights come on for MARK's line.

MARK. If only they would have known before it all started. Where would they be today if it hadn't started at all? If they wanted it this way, why am I so actively involved? It was a different time, a different people. Look at us today; where have we been and how far have we really come? Far enough to say, "No," or far enough to say, "Yes"? The answers are still rising in the smoke and filling the sky with an ugly cloud, and we still look up and cannot read.

Vietnam: Perspectives and Performance

UPSTAGE

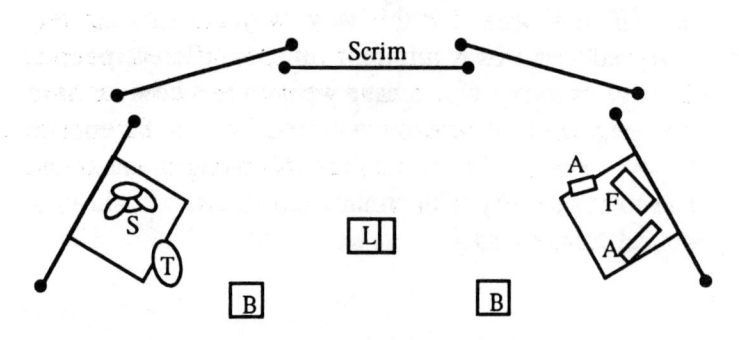

Scrim

DOWNSTAGE

Lights up 1/2. Short musical interlude. "Price of Freedom," by Britt Small and Festival. Downstage right block moves to upstage right, off upstage corner of platform. Full lights.

SURVIVING THE EDGE

CHRIS.   I guess I was willing to do it again. I thought this was the biggest bunch of insanity I'd ever seen in my life, because here we were defending a country against itself, who didn't really want to be defended, because the ARVN didn't really want to fight. They'd rather let us fight. The people back in the United States didn't want us there, although the government wanted us there. It just didn't make any sense to me at all. Why were we there? What were we doing?

I went over there, "Yeah, I'm going to protect us and fight Communism." After I got there a while, I saw just the pure insanity of it. There was Hamburger Hill, Dak To.... I wasn't at these places, but I saw what was going on. I mean, the 101st Airborne ran up and down this hill 15 times. For what reason? To turn the hill right back over to the enemy as soon as they took it. Because they were Airborne, because they needed to take this hill, they killed how many thousand guys? For what? They gave it back to them anyway. It didn't make any sense to me.

So after I'd been in Tet for a while, I started numbing my mind. I got back...I just wanted to make up for the lost time, the time I lost while I was in the service, you know. I look and see all the people I know, and they've got nice houses and I'm not really jealous of them, but I think, "Hey, if I were here, I could have been doing that. I could be looking forward to that."

But anyway, I know for a fact that I've got a world of experience that they will never have in their whole lives, and that's what gets me to feel better about it, knowing the experience that I've had...that 75% of my graduating high school class will never be able to get. You know, all this gets your "pet vet" thing. It was kind of nice to get some respect. Like everyone says, "It's ten years too late." I care...I care about them, the vets in the vet group. Anything I can do to help, I'll help them. Anyone else can go to hell in a handbasket, for all I care.

MARK.   I've seen the way they've treated guys. Not so much me, but I've seen a lot of guys...because they are vets, they can't get things together, because they got problems, and depression and stuff and no one understands or wants to understand. They defended this country, and they're sitting there now—in '59 to '75 they were doing another job, and they can't get another job right now because of Vietnam. If they can't help a service man out, if they can't help a Vet out and give him a job, then I have no time for them.

There have been situations where they could have hired a Vet and didn't do it. You take a guy, and he's got—yeah, he may not have all the technical terms, but by God, he's got military training. He knows how to follow instructions, take control, and do the job—no matter what the job is. That right there...you can go to college for twenty years and never get that kind of training. And I see it every day.

DAVE.   I was wondering who'd be there waiting for me. I expected my wife. We had heard some of the stuff that was going on back in the States—how the bigger people were whining about, "Hell with you guys, die if you want. We're going to stay here, we ain't going. We're not going this year." We heard about that. "You baby killers. You'd kill anybody, won't you?" So, I didn't know what to expect.

JASON.   My family shared that they felt uncomfortable. They didn't know what to do about it. It's obviously been a long war that people now felt like they weren't going to support. They led me to believe that it was something they would just as soon avoid. If they could talk about the weather or plants or crops, if we needed rain, those were the topics, more so than—I hadn't gone on to college; that came up a couple of times. So, after five, six years, I went back to school.

MATHEW. The GI Bill. "Oh, yes. I'm a Vet. Give me money." I wasted my education. I have to admit that most of the people I'm around accept me for what I am, and since I joined the rap group, my life has been on a spiral. The rap group is great. I wouldn't be where I am without it. I went through probably sixty jobs since I got out of the service. I work maybe two, three weeks, get mad and quit. And I was out of employment, and out of school, and all that, and I just decided it was time to settle my tail down and do something I like to do. I got into this job and it's answered every question I had. Everything I want to do for right now. So, it's self-fulfilling work. Getting myself to that point was the hardest thing to do.

SAM. It was hard getting back into the flow of society. What to wear. It had been...after three years, you don't, you know...just nothing seemed to fit me anymore. Everything was old, and I didn't...I always liked to dress well. I was—for lack of a better term—I was an Ivy League-type dresser, you know. Sharp stuff. I wasn't the blue-jean type. I don't know if that's good or bad. I liked that good, clean look. So, here I am. Right away I was confused. "How do I go about this?"

Usually the first ones who could tell you how to dress were the girls and that—I was still apprehensive about that. That was a hard thing to get back into—dating—because the only thing I had to talk about was

Vietnam: Perspectives and Performance

Vietnam. I was...I was at a loss, other than that or the sports page, and that doesn't last long, only five or ten minutes.

MYRA. Well...I'd do it again. In spite of everything. I mean, if I were called upon to go, I would do it again. That's just the way I feel about it, even though I know more about Vietnam, having been there and...since I got back, you learn more about all the politics that took place and everything. In spite of it...in spite of it...I'm no better that anybody else and I love my country. And I'd do it again!

DAVE. I'm proud of it. If I wasn't married right now, and if I didn't have any children, I'd love to go back there and try to get the POWs...'cause I'm sure we've got them there. And I'd like to get about a dozen guys that are just down...just hunters. And this is no—I'd love to go back, because I'd be a sniper. We'd all be. You know, I think there's a way we could get some out, and that's what I'd like to do.

MATHEW. I was a 19-year-old who came back as a 40-year-old. I grew up awful fast. I lost my childhood.

CHRIS. I have some regrets that we were unable to clearly determine the purpose for it so everybody could listen up and say, "Hey, we weren't all that wrong." There were family structures, there were these people we were talking about...you didn't grow to love them, but you respected their culture. They had family religions. It was passed traditionally down, and when the Communists came, the young of that regime destroyed all that; literally wiped it off the face of the earth, and that's no longer there.

So, I kind of felt today that I would never want to do anything similar to that again under those circumstances, and I would not let our government commit us to foreign soil without a very clear statement to the purpose or goal. I feel that's where we have been let down by politicians.

MYRA. A French-trained, very highly-respected, excellent physician and I were visiting one day and a psychiatrist was saying—we were talking about the American-Vietnamese relationship—and he asked that when we leave, what will we have left for the people? He looked me square in the eye and said, "You have left them nothing." And I asked him to explain that further.

This guy was real honest and very, very, deeply hurt; and he said, "The Americans come, they do things for us and to us, but they don't give us any respect. They don't give us any real control. And so when the Americans are gone...there's nothing there." And I think that is very accurate. We were extremely arrogant with the Vietnamese. We did not respect their race; we did not respect their culture; we had no understanding of the pressure on them.

MATHEW. There's a big, glowing difference between the Vietnam War and the rest of the wars this country's been involved in, and that is the education factor. You know, mostly the men and women who served in Vietnam had a high comprehension level.

My biggest problem with Vietnam was—I don't feel so much my effort in the war was useless; it's that I feel that I wasted my time fighting for who's left here. Okay, I did it. I went over and fought, thinking that I was protecting people like Abby Hoffman. These privileged groups of people that didn't have to go, for either money or for other reasons, you know. You'll hear a lot of so-called "educated people" types say, "Well, I just didn't want to die." Just the thought— being able to feel that way. "I don't want to go, so I'm not going." To have that ability to be able to do that.

It's ridiculous when you stop to think about it, because most of the guys in Vietnam never had that opportunity to say, "Well, I don't want to go."

JASON. Nobody, including the President of the United States, has the power or should even consider sending people to die unless it's an extremely just cause. We're talking about if we're having a war on. They ruin too many people's lives. They're willing to commit people to dying in the battlefields, but they're not willing to pick up the pieces. Yeah, it's fine that I went. I get 30% disability for Post-Traumatic Stress Disorder because I'm a weird dude, all right. I guess I'm different than everybody else who went, but they basically shattered everyone, each one of us...individual lives, and they don't want to account for that.

MARK.   Years later. I'm shaking now. (*Pause.*) On the other hand, I'm glad I know I can do it. (*Laughs.*) It's just a hell of an experience. I have no qualms about killing...it's just who I kill and...you're forever relating to someone else. It's part of the war that doesn't go away.

You know, everybody's got a temper—thank you, mine's under control very well; it always has been—but there's always a time when somebody will say something to you and get...you know, they'll put the edge on you...you know, everybody gets frustrated, you know, something stupid...like a clerk in a C-Store. They've got to count the change four times, and you go, "Geez, you're the stupidest human being that God let live. You shouldn't be here anymore," and, "I could just kill you!" and Bingo! You know? And you think to yourself, "Whoa, are you still sick?" (*Laughs.*)

And then I'll calm myself down. I mean, someone will make you mad for some stupid reason, like, you'll

Iowa Stories: The Vietnam Experience

see some guys get mad at an umpire at a baseball game. And it just—I bet you a million dollars the guy's never had an umpire's mask on and been behind the plate. Yet he can stand there and criticize the guy all day. He's...to me, you know, the guy ought to be snuffed. He doesn't deserve to live unless he's done it. That's a hard thing to live with, to keep yourself from thinking those stupid things.

DAVE. Well, I try to forget about it. I try to never bring it up, actually, but it stays with you. I don't go to rap sessions. As a matter of fact, I have a strong mind and will to get ahead, and I don't want to look back. So I don't let it control me, because to me, Vietnam was a bad experience, very bad. I want to sort of forget it, and I want to join the people that were there. We don't talk about Vietnam too much, but we talk about helping each other, and I think that is very important.

SAM. You know, life is ludicrous. This existence that we call life here to me is nothing but a joke. That's basically what it is. I look at everyone in the great real world, and I laugh in their faces because they're stupid, you know. I'm supposed to go out and function every day. The only difference between me and the rest of the world is my nerves are totally wired. I'm wired, okay? I'm wired 24 hours a day, 52 weeks a year, and I'm supposed to go out and function like everybody else, because everybody else says, "Well, those things happen." You know, "That was a war and you've got to go on with your life." But you never do. When you've been in a war, you never go on with your life. It's over.

MYRA. I think that the thing that has been lost in all the issues around Vietnam is that the GIs today have been soldiers because that was their job. They were trying very hard to do their job. They wanted to do their job

– 71 –

the best they could. It was impossible to do that. It wasn't their fault. They did the best they could under extremely difficult situations. And I think this nation needs to look at itself and think, "Why did we put those people in that position?"

MATHEW. They really stereotyped the Vietnam veteran. Christians that went to Vietnam that maybe weren't even in conflict, Christians were labeled as baby-rapers, as murderers and drug addicts and stuff like that. The typical Vietnam veteran is stereotyped...is scorned. They had human waste thrown on them...and spit on and stuff like that. Our country should never be divided. We went through the Civil War and we went through the Vietnam War looking down on each other for our opinions, but we should never be divided and looking down on each other like that.

CHRIS. It's a blackball. What happens is you get into the '80s, and we're into the era of open-mindedness, the '80s. We're moving forward, we've got Yuppies, God knows what. The problem is, we're all too old now. We were too young and crazy, then we were in the middle and we're all getting counseling, and now we're all—some of us are coming around and getting our lives squared away. But who the hell wants to hire a 42-year-old graduate when they got 21-year-olds just waiting? So, we're too old now, you see. I know how this system works.

TERESA. I still have anxiety. It just seems like something...if you're with somebody, it's never quite as bad as when you're by yourself. And having somebody to relate with...[if I had someone in Vietnam]...it would have helped a lot. Not having that always felt like an extra deprivation to me...that I didn't have somebody. There was a lot of jealousy that existed if I spent too

Iowa Stories: The Vietnam Experience

much time...I mean, if I ate three meals a day with the same individual...there were repercussions on that. And so, it made it difficult.

MARK. I had to come to terms with it. It was...sometime in 1982 that I—it all started before then, but it came to a head. My wife—there was a rap group set up in Waterloo...I don't know what year...I think it was 1981...or maybe '82...I don't know. It's a Vietnam veterans support group.

I remember the first meeting I went to. I found out that my wife had been going to the women's—the wives and girlfriends of Vietnam veterans had a group, too, at that time. She'd been going to that for maybe a couple of months and was trying to figure out how to get me to go—not to her group, to the men's group. She evidently had seen—she saw me slowly killing myself with booze and neglecting my family. I had been doing it a long time and I hadn't realized it. I'm getting better at that.

Anyway, the day I finally went...she dropped hints a lot—had a guy call me a couple of times. And, you know, to me the war just wasn't bothering me; that wasn't it, you know? I just—Good Time Charlie. I had nothing to—I didn't have a drinking problem. Well, I did.

A friend of mine got killed. I had been at his funeral and about half-way through the wake I was getting pretty sloshed with a bunch of friends of mine. We were sitting around talking about him. Oh, I s'pose it was 7:30. I just said, "I'm going to go." So I went down; found out one of the rules about being there was you're supposed to be there sober, so I felt a little apprehensive about staying. You know, they had me in there, they were going to keep me there. So after that, I started going back regularly and started talking about the real war. Through a couple of fellows I met there...became real close friends with...they just...they helped me. I talked about things that were bothering me, not only Vietnam, but life in general; my failures and successes and that sort of thing. Prior to that...I had been involved in other things, but my involvement seemed to be an excuse for drinking. They didn't drink, so it was a good place for me to go...it was a sober experience.

But since that time, Vietnam has taken up a lot of my life. It's always been a positive thing. We built the Vietnam Memorial in Waterloo. That was a...that sure opened up the war for us. I mean, we talked to everybody. We contacted the families of all the dead that are listed on the monument. It was a cleansing experience, so to speak. There wasn't a story we didn't hear, a tear we didn't catch. It was...it was bittersweet, but my God, it was the most...to me it is one of the most important things I have ever done in my life.

SAM.   I have a boy. I asked him if he wanted to go with me to the Vietnam Veterans Reunion. I said to him, "This was the big one."

But he said to me, "But, Dad, you lost."

I said, "We didn't lose; we just quit." Just think... even little kids think that. We didn't lose; we just quit. I knew the minute they started pulling those troops out of there, it was gone. It was over. If they would have just let us attack! You can't win a war without attacking. They wouldn't hardly let us go into Cambodia. If they would have let us land in North Vietnam and taken away their resources, we could have won the thing.

JENNIFER. I learned to relax in Vietnam, to take things as they came. It gave me some confidence that I didn't have before. I figured if I could go through that, I could do almost anything. A belonging, a sense of belonging.

Iowa Stories: The Vietnam Experience

CHRIS. Why do we still have POWs there? I don't understand why we can't make an all-out military effort to go back and militarily run through that country and get our POWs. They ought to come up with something. If the Vietnamese are threatened with a military attack, they will come up with something to get those POWs out of there. I don't understand why we can't use our military strength to say, "Give them to us or we're coming after them. Period."

MATHEW. The first couple of times, I told them everything. I didn't leave anything out. I blew everything out. I didn't stop. I told them everything that was bothering me. And it...that became my second family. I love it. They are a tremendous group that helped me a lot. And I just wouldn't talk much about it with my wife. She asked me quite a few questions, and I just told the facts, and that's about it.

MYRA. I find that I don't have to push anything anymore, I don't have to try to tell people things anymore. They usually come and ask, especially this new generation of kids. They are so...interested. A lot of them have gone through fathers, uncles, older brothers... people who are having problems. They don't understand and they want to understand. They're very curious.

TERESA. These young men and women gave so much and got so little. Many gave their lives. They're due every respect. Before we get involved in another conflict such as that, we need a stated goal in mind. We went in there not really knowing, with no actual goal down the road. Before we commit American troops again, let's have it more identified. Let's get the country behind us. A war is a war. Lives were lost...the flower of American youth...especially in Vietnam. They gave so much. Let's have a little bit of it back.

Music comes up. Any type of patriotic music will do. Cast is divided on both sides of the stage. From stage right and left, two soldiers appear. One a combat soldier and the other in dress uniform. They move to center stage in front of the scrim. The combat soldier takes a protective position near the floor. They are presenting the American Flag. The cast comes to attention, facing the soldiers and flag, salute the flag, then turn and during the rest of the song they mix with the audience. They shake hands with audience members and welcome the Vets home. At the end of the song the cast members move back to the stage area and assume their positions before mixing with the audience. Combat soldier rises and music fades. Lights slowly fade to black. "The Wall," by Britt Small and Festival plays as the audience exits.

THE END

VIETNAMESE CHESS
by
Chris Ellsbury & Jennifer Terry

Vietnamese Chess

The following copyrighted materials appear in VIETNAMESE CHESS *with permission. In some instances, material has been edited or altered; however, for readability, editing markers have been omitted. For the complete work, please consult these sources:*

DEAR AMERICA: LETTERS HOME FROM VIETNAM
Bernard Edelman, ed. New York: W.W. Norton, 1986. Used with permission from Bernard Edelman for the Vietnam Veterans Memorial Commission.
"Letter Home" submitted by David Bowman.
"The Victors" submitted by Barry Reeves.
"Letters from Pleiku" by Major Michael Davis O'Donnell.
"Untitled" by Major Michael Davis O'Donnell.

THE COMPLETE GREEK DRAMA, vol. I & II
Whitney J. Oates and Eugene O'Neill, Jr., eds. New York: Random House, 1938. All are within public domain or within free-use limits.
Agamemnon by Aeschylus, trans. EDA Morshead.
Choephori by Aeschylus, trans. EDA Morshead.
Eumenides by Aeschylus, trans. EDA Morshead.
Prometheus Bound by Aeschylus, trans. Paul Elmer More.
Philoctetes by Sophocles, trans. Thomas Francklin.
Oedipus the King by Sophocles, trans. RC Jebb.
The Bacchae by Euripides, trans. Gilbert Murray.

VISIONS OF WAR, DREAMS OF PEACE
Lynda Van Devanter and Joan A. Furey, eds. New York: Warner, 1990. Used with permission from Lynda Van Devanter only for publication in this volume. For information regarding performance rights to this material, please contact the Association for Textual Study and Production.
"Some Days" by Joan A. Furey.
"The Vietnam Vet" by Norma J. Griffiths.
"Even Now" by Bernadette Harrod.

TASK FORCE OMEGA
"Dear America" was taken from a free-use publication of Task Force Omega.

Introduction

During our "Tour of Duty" in Marilyn's production, we met hundreds of Vietnam veterans and their families and were struck by the amazing stories they told to us, some about what happened to them during the war years, and some about what has happened since. While these stories varied from humorous anecdotes to heart-wrenching tragedies, the variety did reveal to us a unifying principle: war experiences function in the realms of the extreme. From intense adrenalin-laden battles and artillery barrages to quiet boring stretches of sun-bathing and basic maintenance; from good times and parties with war buddies to the violent deaths of close friends; the veteran was placed in a position to confront the outermost boundaries of human experience.

One of our first thoughts upon hearing these accounts was that these people were, at the time of the Vietnam Conflict, within our own age group. The thought of being 18-24 years-old and living through such a range of experience instantly humbled us. The question, "How could someone survive this?" reverberated in our minds. It was then that the wife of a Vietnam veteran approached us and said, "That was fine, but when are you going to tell our side of story?" These questions prompted our research.

Stress and coping mechanisms which frequently occur in Vietnam veterans and their spouses are not unlike those which exist in any other group or individual. However, the more immediate impact of the Vietnam legacy on the lives of these people has had a tendency to magnify both the effects of the stress instigators and the methods employed to cope with these stresses.

Many veterans have felt used and abandoned by their government and by their fellow Americans, believing that their completed contribution to the war effort made them wholly expendable in some overshadowing bureaucratic game. It is like a game of chess, with different forces moving across the board into positions where they could attack or protect. This is the image with which we decided to "play" in the script. Pawns are the most expendable pieces on the board and are easy targets for the opposing pieces to remove from the game; therefore, we crafted the metaphor with the idea of the players as the Pawns.

The methods of coping with stress, and the stresses themselves, may come from a variety of sources and manifest themselves in a multitude of forms. From our research, we discovered that the veterans tend to employ a specific style of coping, and even though the actual mechanism may be the same (alcohol, for example), the rationales for their behavior may come from very different world views or constructs of reality. For the veterans, we came up with three principal groups which easily fit into our chess metaphor. Some people are very concrete, very hands-on, physical types. These characteristics we have embodied in the Rooks. Others rely upon their emotional reactions and their relationships with others. These we represented with the Knights. Still others look at the world intellectually or philosophically and weigh the values or morals of their actions. These come under the guidance of the Bishops.

Since the Queens are the most powerful pieces on the board, they symbolize overall support, which may utilize any of the other styles. Finally, the Kings, whose safety is the concern of the entire board, signify the ideology for which the battle is raised. All of these forces may work for or against the Pawns, that is, for or against the veterans and their families, depending upon which "side" the forces are located on.

We placed two veterans each under the principal influence of either the Rooks, the Knights, or the Bishops. The Queen and King are representative of the nation itself, so we found the Pawns under their jurisdiction to be played best by the wives.

Having the basic character types defined, we poured over forty interviews to seek out statements and stories which conveyed these types. In real life, of course, everyone experiences physical, emotional, intellectual, and philosophical forms of stress and utilizes the mechanisms described above in coping with them. Our characters were created with a "slant" in mind to show how an emphasis upon one system could manifest itself.

In addition to the eight characters playing Pawns in this game of chess, there is another pawn, not in this game, who represents those who were sacrificed in an earlier match, the chess game during the war itself. The Prisoner of War/Missing In Action (POW/MIA) issue is emotionally charged and ever-lingering in most Vietnam veteran circles, and as the "Letter" in the last scene dictates, all Pawns lost in former battles have earned the right to be remembered.

Any game of chess must have those who move the pieces and call the shots, so the dread image of the Fates was easily accessible, and so was the more fearful image of the Furies. Our Chorus, taken primarily from Classical Greek dramas, plays on both levels.

In our production of VIETNAMESE CHESS, we also attempted subtly to unify the recurrent nature of War by bringing in various tokens of other times. The dialogue itself refers to World War II, Korea, and the Persian Gulf; the Greek chorus echoes poetic lines of the Trojan War; the Caller's chess set had medieval battle pieces; and Dave spends the first few scenes reading *All Quiet on the Western Front*. There is a bitter constancy found in war and its effects on humanity. The experiences of our characters can in some way be found throughout the history of soldiers returning home.

NOTES ON STAGING

Our stage consists of a 16x16 foot chessboard with 2x2 foot squares. (For greater movement capabilities, 2.5 or 3 foot squares might be more functional.) The board has four levels, each tier 9" higher than the level in front of it and each having two rows. Five pairs of chess pieces are used so that each side has one King, Queen, Bishop, Knight, and Rook. The checkered board is dark green and dark red, the green representing the coping pieces on the side of the pawns and the red the stress pieces. We did not wish to use black and white since Vietnam was hardly a "black-and-white" issue. Red and green are complementary colors and they represent the green camouflage of the GI and the "communist red" of the opposition.

Upstage from the board there is a raised area with a high pedestal which holds the Caller's chessboard. At either side of the Caller are raised platforms which are the "home bases" for the Movers. The image created is similar to a scale. To the stage right of the board there is a cage with a block or stool. This is the home of the POW/MIA. Down-stage from him is the Enactment Area, to which the Movers lead him for the stories they perform. There are blocks as needed. Props may be easily hidden behind the chessboard.

We did not use slides with our production due to space and time limitations. However, either a slide presentation before the production or various stills used during performance time (especially in the Prologue) could add an intriguing dimension to the production.

Chris Ellsbury & Jennifer Terry
July 1993

Vietnam: Perspectives and Performance

THE CHARACTERS

CALLER

The CALLER is the leader of the chorus. She has supreme control over the board and directs the movements of the pieces via the MOVERS, but has mixed emotions about her vocation. She wears a long, flowing, black gown with a removable veil, and her hair is up in a circle braid with small white and purple flowers.

RED MOVER

The RED MOVER is the most vindictive member of the chorus. She likes her job. She moves the stress pieces into position and takes part in the more negative role-playing. Her specialty is creating nightmares for the PAWNS. She wears a black tunic and tights.

GREEN MOVER

The GREEN MOVER is somewhere between the CALLER and the RED MOVER in her attitude; she dutifully fulfills her job, whether it means well or ill for the PAWNS. She is in charge of moving the coping pieces, since they can play both productive and nonproductive roles for the PAWNS. She also wears a black tunic and tights.

POW/MIA

JOSH, the POW/MIA, is used by the MOVERS for reenactments of the PAWNS' memories. He humbly does the tasks assigned, taking on the persona of whichever soldier the story indicates. He wears a black tunic and black pants.

MATT

MATT was a corpsman in Vietnam. As the KING's ROOK's PAWN, his chief concerns are the physical realities of war:

Vietnamese Chess

caring for the injured. The stresses of war and employment problems at home have resulted in his abuse of alcohol. In Part One, he wears a blue knit shirt, a blue stocking cap, bellbottom jeans, and platform shoes. In Part Two, he wears regular jeans and a military field jacket. He always has his rosary.

CORY

CORY is principally controlled by the KING's KNIGHT. He is caught up in the experience of war, a grunt who became addicted to the "high" of battle. Rather than planning and thinking, Cory reacts and feels. In Part One, he wears cut-off jeans, his military jacket, a T-shirt, and a bandana which he utilizes with his drug paraphernalia: marijuana, cocaine, pills, needles, whatever. He also carries a handgun. In Part Two, he wears jeans and a Vietnam T-shirt.

TODD

TODD is governed primarily by the KING's BISHOP. He was a sergeant in Vietnam, and was responsible for taking care of his men. The question of responsibility is central with him, and the internalization of the stress of war takes its toll on him. He nervously plays with a deck of cards. He wears blue jeans, a blue plaid flannel shirt, and hiking boots in Part One, and a sweatshirt, jeans, and cap in Part Two.

SUZIE

SUZIE is the PAWN of the KING. There is a bit of youthful naivete in her when we first meet her; she has a lot to learn, and she does. Hers is a struggle to mediate between what's best for her, for her children, and for her husband. In the end, she realizes that the relationship cannot go on with safety. She wears a '60s-style jumper in Part One and a high-collared, light-colored sweater with pants in Part Two.

MEGAN

MEGAN is the PAWN of the QUEEN. She has firmly decided that she will stick it out, and that her husband can get better—not necessarily cured, but better. She believes that her relationship with him has a lot to do with his improvement. She wears a housedress and works away on her latchhook in Part One, and wears a simple blouse and pants in Part Two and reads a book about coping with the Vietnam Conflict.

DAVE

DAVE was a REMF in Vietnam: "a rear-echelon motherfucker," as the vets affectionately say. He is the QUEEN's BISHOP's PAWN. The mentality of War is central to him and affects him quite intensely. He wears a tan corduroy suit in Part One, and reads a book. In Part Two, he wears a nice suit and reads the paper.

DARRIN

DARRIN is the PAWN of the QUEEN's KNIGHT. He guarded a base while in Vietnam. His experiences have isolated him from society, and he has had difficulty returning to a world of social interaction. He has a sketch pad and is constantly drawing. He wears a leather vest, a red bandana, a black T-shirt, jeans, and boots throughout the show. He also possesses a handgun and bottles of medication.

SHEILA

SHEILA is the QUEEN's ROOK's PAWN. She, like Matt, dealt with the physical realities of war: nursing the injured. The isolation she experiences as one of the "uncounted" female veterans results in some use of alcohol (not as severe as Matt's). She sadly gazes into a scrapbook, but later she is able to gain expression for her thoughts and feelings through

Vietnamese Chess

her writing. In Part One, she wears a blue flowered shirt, blue bellbottoms, and sandals. In Part Two, she wears a green military field jacket and pants.

ADDITIONAL COSTUMING

A common article of clothing for Vietnam veterans is the POW/MIA bracelet. During the Vietnam Conflict, bracelets were generally a red metal band on which was inscribed the name of the missing person and the details of their disappearance. Today, there are many varieties of POW/MIA bracelets. In costuming Part One, the cast should wear red bracelets, if possible. In Part Two, bracelets and other Vietnam veteran paraphernalia may be varied. (Contact your local Vet Center for information on POW/MIA bracelets.) In addition, dog tags or medals may also be incorporated as common remembrance devices. Because smoking is a very common habit among both veterans and their spouses, cigarettes may be used freely as an additional property for cast members to utilize throughout the performance.

Vietnam: Perspectives and Performance

VIETNAMESE CHESS

Originally performed April 28 – May 1, 1993, at the University of Northern Iowa, Cedar Falls, Iowa.

THE CHORUS

CALLER	Jennifer Nardini
RED MOVER	Ali Jeners
GREEN MOVER	Giao Phan

THE PAWN OF THE:

QUEEN's ROOK, a nurse	Sheila Rae Sines
QUEEN's KNIGHT, a guard	Darrin Thompson
QUEEN's BISHOP, a REMF	David J. Hall
QUEEN, a wife	Megan Trower
KING, a wife	Suzanne Hilger
KING's BISHOP, a sergeant	Todd H. Hawley
KING's KNIGHT, a grunt	Cory Losenicky
KING's ROOK, a corpsman	Matt Stovall
POW/MIA	Joshua Fouts

CREW

Compilers/Directors	Jennifer Terry
	Chris Ellsbury
Technical Director	Scott Hansen
Assistant Technical Director	Jim Riley
Stage Manager/Audio	Mark Herbsleb
Lights	Cory Manning
Makeup	Marilyn Shaw
Costumes/Props	Megan Trower
Publicity	Jim Bentley
Coordinator of Interpretation	Phyllis Carlin

Vietnamese Chess

Prologue

Lights rise on the CALLER, who stands in the center of the empty chessboard with the MOVERS at her sides. They are dressed in flowing, black Greek robes.

CALLER. And woe! for him who stands
   Shamed, silent, unreproachful, stretching hands
   That find her not, and sees, yet will not see,
   That his sad fancy, yearning o'er the sea,
   Shall summon and recall, sad with many memories
   The fair cold beauty of each sculptured face.
MOVERS. And when the night is deep,
   Come visions, sweet and sad, and bearing pain
   Of hopings vain.
CALLER. Void.
MOVERS. Void and vain,
   It vanishes away
   On silent wings that roam adown the ways of sleep.
CALLER. Familiar was each face, and dear as life,
   That went unto the war;
   But thither, whence a warrior went of old,
   Doth nought return.
ALL. Only a spear and sword, and ashes in an urn!
CALLER. For the lord of strife
   Sends back to hearts that held them dear
   Scant ashes of warriors, wept with many a tear.
R.MOVER. Light to the hand...
G.MOVER. But heavy to the soul.
R.MOVER. Alas!
CALLER. One cries...
R.MOVER. And yet alas again!

– 89 –

Vietnam: Perspectives and Performance

G.MOVER. Ah woe!
CALLER. Another moans...
G.MOVER. My spouse is slain!
ALL. The death of honour rolled in dust and blood....
CALLER. Such muttered words of bitter mood
  Rise against those who went,
  As deeply and deadly as a curse more loud
  Flung by the coming fate...
MOVERS. Against the sons of carnage
CALLER. Buried as yet in darkness' womb.[1]

> *CALLER signals MOVERS to bring in the PAWNS. R.MOVER lines up MEGAN, DAVE, DARRIN, and SHEILA on the stage-right edge of the board. G.MOVER lines up SUZIE, TODD, CORY, and MATT on the stage-left edge of the board. The MOVERS return to their posts. All PAWNS are dressed in 70s-style clothing. SHEILA holds a scrapbook, DARRIN a sketch pad and pen, DAVE a book, MEGAN her latchhook materials, and TODD a deck of cards.*

SETTING THE BOARD

CALLER. Dear Civilians, Friends, Draft Dodgers, etc.:
  In the very near future, the undersigned will once more be in your midst, dehydrated and demoralized, to take their places again as human beings with the well-known forms of freedom and justice for all; engage in life, liberty, and the somewhat delayed pursuit of happiness. In making your joyous preparations to welcome them back into organized society, you might take certain steps to make allowances for the past twelve months.

Vietnamese Chess

MATT.   In other words, he might be a little Asiatic from Vietnamesitis and Overseasitis, and should be handled with care.

CORY.   Don't be alarmed if he is infected with all forms of rare tropical diseases.

SHEILA.   A little time in the "Land of the Big PX" will cure this malady.

TODD.   Therefore, show no alarm if he insists on carrying a weapon to the dinner table, looks around for his steel pot when offered a chair...

DARRIN.   Or wakes you up in the middle of the night for guard duty.

MATT.   Keep cool at dinner when he pours gravy on his dessert of peaches mixed with Seagrams VO.

TODD.   Pretend not to notice if he acts dazed, eats with his fingers instead of silverware, and prefers C-rations to steak.

DARRIN.   Take it with a smile when he insists on digging up the garden to fill sandbags for the bunker he is building.

CORY.   Be tolerant when he takes his blanket and sheet off the bed and puts them on the floor to sleep on.

DAVE.   Abstain from saying anything about powdered eggs, dehydrated potatoes, fried rice, or ice cream.

MATT.   Do not be alarmed if he should jump up from the dinner table and rush to the garbage can to wash his dish with a toilet brush.

DAVE.   After all, this has been his standard.

TODD.   Also, if it should start raining, pay no attention to him if he pulls off his clothes, grabs a bar of soap and a towel, and runs outdoors for a shower.

DAVE.   When in his daily conversation he utters such things as, "Xin loi," and, "Choi oi," just be patient, and simply leave quickly and calmly if by some chance he

utters, "Didi," with an irritated look on his face, because it means no less than, "Get the hell out of here."
DARRIN. Do not let it shake you up if he picks up the phone and yells, "Sky King forward, Sir," or says, "Roger out," for goodbye or simply shouts, "Working."
CORY. Never ask why the Jones' son held a higher rank than he did.
MATT. And by no means mention the word—
ALL VETS. "Extend."
CORY. Pretend not to notice if at a restaurant he calls the waitress "numbuh 1 girl" and uses his hat as an ashtray.
DAVE He will probably keep listening for "Homeward Bound" to sound off over Armed Forces Radio-Saigon. If he does, comfort him, for he is still reminiscing.
SHEILA. Be especially watchful when he is in the presence of women—
ALL MALE VETS. Especially a beautiful woman.
DARRIN. Above all, keep in mind that beneath that tanned and rugged exterior there is a heart of gold.
TODD. (The only thing of value he has left.)
SHEILA. Treat her with kindness, tolerance...
MATT. And an occasional fifth of good liquor...
DAVE And you will be able to rehabilitate that which was once (and now a hollow shell) the happy-go-lucky guy you knew and loved.
SHEILA. Last but not least, send no more mail to the APO...
MATT. Fill the ice box with beer...
DARRIN. Get the civvies out of the mothballs...
CORY. Fill the car with gas...
TODD. And get the women and children off the street...
ALL VETS. BECAUSE THE KID IS COMING HOME![2]

As MOVERS place PAWNS into their starting positions, music and/or slides may be used.

Vietnamese Chess

Opening Positions

DOWNSTAGE

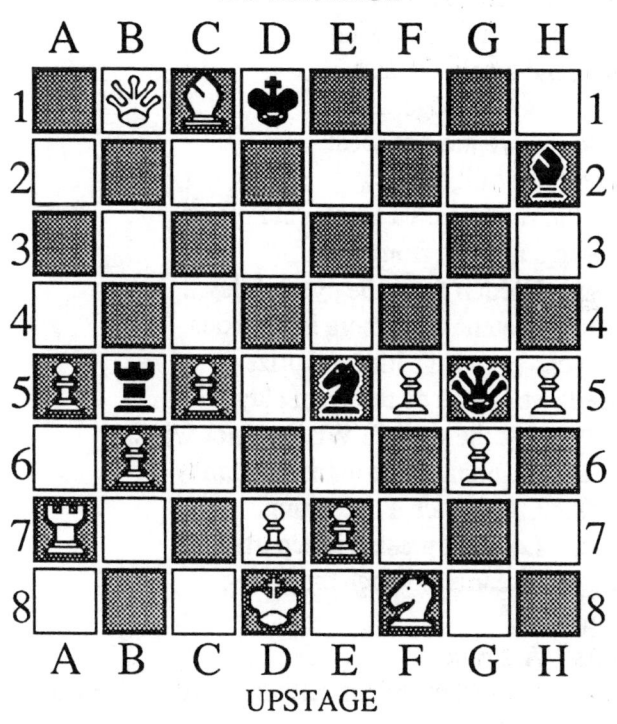

UPSTAGE

Moves in This Scene

	RED		**GREEN**	
1.	Rook	B5-B1	Todd	C5-C4
2.	Queen	G5-D2	Rook	A7-A6
3.	Queen	D2-G5	Dave	F5-F4
4.	Queen	G5-F6	Suzie	D7-D6

Chorus

CALLER.   A strait pitiless mind
   Is death unto godliness;
   And to feel in human kind
   Life, and a pain the less.
ALL.   Knowledge...
CALLER.   ...we are not foes!
   I seek thee diligently;
   But the world with a great wind blows,
   Shining, and not from thee.[3]
MOVERS.   Hidden from the eyes of day...
CALLER.   Watchers are there in the skies,
   That can see man's life, and prize
   Deeds well done by things of clay.
R.MOVER.   But the world's Wise are not wise...
G.MOVER.   Claiming more than mortal may.
MOVERS.   Life is such a little thing.
CALLER.   Lo, their present is departed,
   And the dreams to which they cling
   Come not.[4]
MOVERS.   A strain...
CALLER.   Unbidden and unwelcome, thrills mine ear,
   Oracular of pain.
   Not as of old upon my bosom's throne
   Sits Confidence, to spurn
   Such fears, like dreams we know not to discern.
MOVERS.   Old...
CALLER.   Old and grey long since the time has grown,
   And now mine eyes and not another's see
   Their safe return.
   Yet none the less in me
   The inner spirit sings a boding song.

Vietnamese Chess

ALL.   Sings the Furies' strain...
CALLER.   ...and seeks, and seeks in vain,
  To hope and to be strong!
G.MOVER.   How oft the famine-stricken field
  Is saved by God's large gift, the new year's yield!
R.MOVER.   But blood of man once spilled,
  Once at his feet shed forth, and darkening the plain...
ALL.   ...nor chant nor charm can call it back again.[5]

> RED: *Rook B5-B1; Rook takes Queen.*
> *G.MOVER puts a block in MEGAN's square for her to sit on, then gives a wine bottle and glass to SHEILA. Lights. G.MOVER lets JOSH out of his cage and leads him to the enactment area for TODD's story. G.MOVER sits on a block and reads a magazine.*

OPENING MOVES

TODD.   When I came home, they took us to Okinawa... one of the nicest things that happened to me, and I'll never forget it. This girl sat down next to me, and I never smelled anything so good in my life as she did, and I was just—then I knew how bad I'd stunk. And I hadn't sat next to a Caucasian girl in months, and I was just like a high school sophomore.
MATT.   I can remember how strange the stewardess looked compared to the Oriental women—you get used to looking at a certain thing—and I saw the American stewardess and I found out I was still somewhat alive!
TODD.   She was just the most beautiful creature I had ever seen in my life. And she smelled so good, and I stunk so bad. And I was so embarrassed; I remember drawing my arms in like this.

Vietnam: Perspectives and Performance

MATT. I think in my mind, the thought of being with a woman—not just sexually—that really represented everything that was home.

TODD. But I couldn't help myself, and I finally leaned over and I said...

JOSH. You smell so good.

TODD. And she said—she had a southern accent, I'll never forget—she said...

G.MOVER. Thank you, honey.

TODD. And I tell you my heart just went budda-blam-budda-blam. It did. To have her say, "Thank you, honey," like that. That was one of the most sensual experiences I have ever had, just to tell her, "You smell so good."

G.MOVER leads JOSH back to the cage.

MATT. The thought of family or wife—that was home. That sort of became symbolic of everything you wanted to get back to.

GREEN: TODD C5-C4.

TODD. When I got off the plane, I was hit in the face with a bag of dog shit.

SUZIE. With my own family and friends, I was proud of him! But to the outside world you didn't say anything. You learned early on there were people who asked, "Why didn't he go to Canada?"

SHEILA. I was a little frightened. Happy I was coming back, and yet Vietnam had become the known, and I was coming back to the unknown.

SUZIE. They'd say, "Why did he join the Marines, for God's sake? He shouldn't be over there!"

SHEILA. Knowing the sentiment that existed stateside, I wondered how I'd react if someone spit on me.

SUZIE. I was the one at the airport to greet him coming home. As the plane landed, I see these people are out

Vietnamese Chess

there putting out this red carpet. I said, "What the...?" Just for a flash I thought, "This was for him!"

SHEILA.   We landed at three a.m. in Oakland and I took a military shuttle to my next plane, so I had very little contact that way.

FREEZE—RED: Queen G5-D2.

SUZIE.   All these people are disembarking from the plane and are all going around the red carpet, and he was about the last one off the plane. He charges right down the middle of that thing! Then after he got off the plane, here comes Art Linkletter. He was a TV personality at the time who was there to talk to the protesters. It was kind of ironic because people really should have been spitting on him and calling him names.

MATT.   When I came back, there were demonstrators at the airport throwing things, and they tried to keep me out of that. They told me not to wear my uniform. They said I'd be "more comfortable."

SUZIE.   That carpet should have been for my husband.

MATT.   And like an idiot, I didn't wear it. To my everlasting shame.

SUZIE.   The day after he came home, he took all his clothes out in the backyard and his military duffel bag and burned them all. He kept only his medals and his papers. He burned the rest. He just wanted none of it around.

MATT.   I'll never forgive myself for doing that.

FREEZE--GREEN: Rook A7-A6; RED: Queen D2-G5. G.MOVER gives a bottle of whiskey to MATT.

MEGAN.   Right after he got home, the family thought we should have this huge reunion, you know, to celebrate his coming home. It didn't quite sound like a good idea to me, but they were adamant about it. So we're at my parents' cabin on the river, all of us, waiting for him to show up.

DARRIN. I didn't want to say anything about it to my mother. It's just something you don't really want to expose them to.

MEGAN. Now, Mom always had wind chimes on the porch, and there was one right in the middle of the porch in front of the door. So when he showed up and walked in, his head just brushed against the wind chime and it rang. And like that! he was on the floor flat out. We just stood there.

DARRIN. And at the same time, you know you'll go insane if you keep it all in.

MEGAN. I wrote it off at the time to just coming home, but looking back, I should have seen it as a sign of things to come.

DAVE It was during basic training where they put you on the field with a bayonet and you're ordered to scream the motto of the bayoneters, which is "To Kill Without Mercy." So here you are out there screaming, "Kill, kill, kill!" and going after your fellows with bayonets. It was kind of fun. And of course either a rabbi, or a minister, or a priest was standing on the podium with the drill sergeant giving you his blessing while you are out there killing. So you have state and church, but then the military controls the Chaplain's Corps and they can order the chaplains to go out there and give their blessing—"Kill for Christ." "Kill for Moses." "Kill for Buddha."

DARRIN. My first Sunday back, she had me in full dress uniform so she could show me off to all of her friends at church. I went along with it because that's what she wanted.

GREEN: DAVE F5-F4.

Vietnamese Chess

DAVE   All values given me by Sunday school and Protestantism were not the values I had operated under in Vietnam. It was "kill or be killed."

TODD.   I used to hunt a lot before I went over there, and that's kind of how I had to think about it—that it was deer hunting.

DAVE   It was "be an animal" in the sense of a mouse running through the room knowing the cat was waiting. So the mentality in war is always waiting for the cat, knowing it's there. And that hyperalertness is what separates the jungle from civilization.

TODD.   In Vietnam it was never human blood, it was always deer blood.

DAVE   The hyperalertness requires so much energy that everything is here...now...immediate. Response. And culture is possible only when you get rid of that necessity for perpetual alertness and redirect your energy toward whatever it is we do in time.

TODD.   I'd just got back and pheasant season had started.

CORY.   One minute I was carrying a gun in the jungle in Vietnam, and twenty-four hours later I was carrying a bag off an airplane in Iowa. And that was it.

TODD.   I'm a traditional guy. I'm from Iowa. My dad was alive yet, and my brother, and so I decided, "We're going to go pheasant hunting."

CORY.   If a car backfired, you wanted to grab a gun. They weren't deprogramming anybody. I always carry a weapon of some kind; I never feel okay without one. There was no debriefing, ever.

DAVE   We were animals in that we were responding to the cat lurking, ready to pounce. Ears open, eyes open, because if you're not alert, you die. You're in the jungle. You're a creature. But at the same time, you have humanity.

CORY. And there was no welcome home. Ever.
FREEZE—RED: Queen G5-F6.
G.MOVER lets JOSH out of the cage, and they join R.MOVER in the enactment area for TODD's story. They carry shotguns. R.MOVER portrays TODD's father and G.MOVER portrays his brother.

TODD. ...and I had this old double-barreled shotgun that I'd had for a hundred years. I load this sucker up and we're going along and I'm talking to my dad, and we hadn't gone a hundred yards and this pheasant moved and it was probably 10 feet away—I'd only been out of Vietnam a couple of months—and I wheeled on it with both barrels, you know, from the hip, and Boom! both barrels and just disintegrated the thing. And my brother's standing there going...

G.MOVER. Jesus!

TODD. And giving me a whole bunch of shit.

CORY. I put my mother through living hell.

TODD. And my old man, he just walks over and picks up this poor disgusting pheasant and my dad looked at me—of course he was in WW II in the Navy—and Dad looked at me and he said, "I think you got it."

JOSH. Yeah.

TODD. He said, "Little quick, aren't ya?"

JOSH. Yeah.

TODD. He said, "Are you gonna load that again?"

JOSH. I don't think so.

TODD. He said, "Okay, we'll just keep on going." That was the last time I ever went hunting.

MOVERS return JOSH to his cage.

CORY. I was 18 years old at the time. I had 30 days leave, and of those 30 days I think I was sober 14; the rest I was blotto drunk or high.

Vietnamese Chess

SUZIE. During WW II, in *Better Homes and Gardens* and *Woman's Day*, they had articles about how to treat your husbands or fiances coming home, but there was never an article for us. They got home, and it was hard.

CORY. Sleep all day, take a shower, go back to the tavern; that's all I was doing.

SUZIE. He was gone a lot. He was gone at night a lot. He'd say, "I'm going fishing," or, "I'm going for a drive," or, "I need to get outta here."

CORY. It was always a lot of restlessness. I was trying to replicate the same adrenalin high that I had there. I missed that rush, that adrenalin high. It was incredible.

SUZIE. But, I would say he was gone probably three-fourths of the time—just gone til very late at night. I basically raised the kids myself—very hard at times.

CORY. I got a new car, a new fast car, and I drove everywhere at 90 mph. I was trying to replicate that adrenalin. It just wasn't possible here, but I tried to stay on that level.

SUZIE. There were times I was glad he was gone. Sometimes it was easier than to put up with him.

CORY. A lot of people couldn't keep up with that. I was bored, so I had to go out and look for trouble to get into.

SUZIE. I did everything for him! He was up at the tavern, and I was home with the kids. We never went anywhere. But, it made me stronger because I knew I could do it.

GREEN: SUZIE D7-D6.

CORY. I realized that if I kept this up, I'd probably end up in jail, or get a dishonorable discharge, so I might as well go back to what I knew. And I reupped and went back to Vietnam as quick as I could.

OPENING POSITIONS

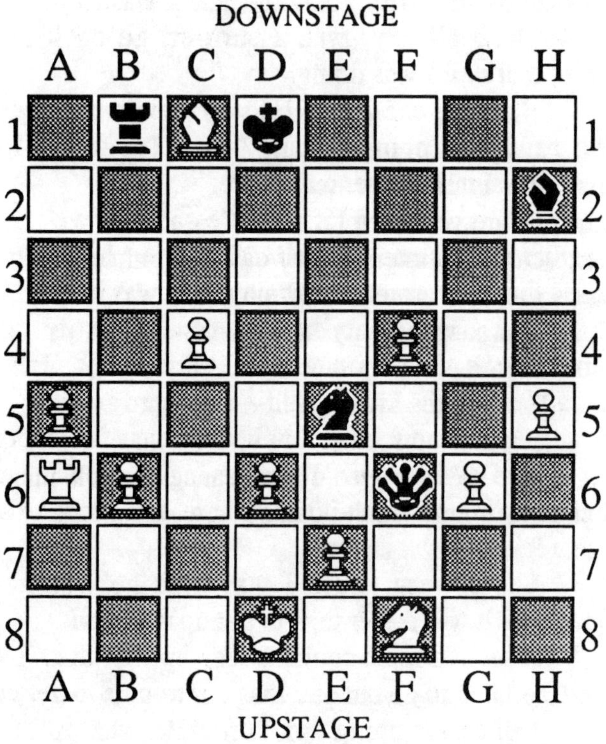

MOVES IN THIS SCENE

	RED		**GREEN**	
1.	Knight	E5-D7	Todd	C4-C3
2.	Rook	B1-B3	Bishop	C1-E3
3.	Bishop	H2-G3	Darrin	G6-G5
4.	Knight	D7-C5	Sheila	H5-H4

Vietnamese Chess

The stage is in halflight. The PAWNS lie down on the board to sleep, except for SHEILA and MATT, who both sit with bottle in hand and stare off the side of the board.

CHORUS

CALLER. Justice doth mark
 With scales that swiftly sway,
 Some that are yet in light...
MOVERS. Others in interspace of day and night...
CALLER. Till Fate arouse them, stay...
R.MOVER. And some are lapped in night
 Where all things are undone.
G.MOVER. On the life-giving lap of Earth
 Blood hath flowèd forth...
CALLER. And now the seed of vengeance clots the plain...
 Unmelting, uneffaced the stain.
MOVERS. Visions, ghastly clear,
 Bearing a blast of wrath from realms below...
CALLER. And stiffening each rising hair with dread,
 Came out of dream-land Fear,
 And, loud and awful, bade...
MOVERS. The shriek ring out at midnight's witching hour.
CALLER. And brooded, stern with woe,
 Above the inner house.
 And seers inspired did read the dream an oath,
 Chanting aloud...
ALL. ...in realms below
 The dead are wroth.
 Against their slayers yet their ire doth glow.
CALLER. Lo, when man's force doth ope
 The virgin doors, there is nor cure nor hope
 For what is lost.

MOVERS. It were in vain.
CALLER. Hiding my face within my robe, fain
Of tears, and chilled with frost of hidden pain.[6]

> CALLER *regretfully gestures to* R.MOVER, *who sneaks onto the board. Crickets are heard in the background.* R.MOVER *pauses to make some mystical hand movements around the* RED *Knight, then looms over* TODD's *sleeping figure. She gestures above him, then she and* CALLER *sharply point to* JOSH *who, as a spotlight grows on him, rises in his cage, grabs the bars, and calls to* TODD.

JOSH. I don't want to go.

> TODD's *eyes pop open but he doesn't move.* R.MOVER *proudly dances away for the next move. Light fades on cage.* G.MOVER *brings a calculator and some bills to* SUZIE.
> RED: *Knight E5-D7.*

PLAYING GAMES

DARRIN. The advice given to me by relatives or anyone else was, "You did a real good job; now get on with your life, and get to work right now." That's kinda hard to do.

MEGAN. He was very negative about the military—the authority especially—a lot more negative than I remember from his letters. Very untrusting.

DARRIN. My older brother, he was six years older than I, and he had always sort of been a role model for me. He had been in the service—he was in the Navy—and he wanted me to go back and serve another tour because

Vietnamese Chess

there wasn't anything going on here and it was the "patriotic" thing to do.

CORY.   On my second tour, I could tell that the morale over there was really dropping. Nobody cared anymore, including me. That's when I began using the drugs.

MEGAN.   In the military's wisdom, they took these guys who had been to Vietnam to Chicago to be in an honor guard for inner city kids who'd died. He had never been to a Black funeral—especially at that time. The Black parishes tended to be real outward about showing their grief. It just drove him crazy. He hated it. It was just too much for him.

DARRIN.   It finally got to the point that I said, "Why don't you go on over there and I'll stay here with your wife." He didn't like that idea, but he was a flag-waver and still is. He didn't understand the war. It was much different for him being in the Navy than for me living in the jungle for a year. Even he couldn't grasp what happened to me.

CORY.   Started off in Vietnam, you could buy a $10 cap of heroin, 98%, about as big around as your finger—that's more than a gram for 10 bucks. Here in the States, that would be about $100 to $200. So, if you had a two-cap habit in Vietnam, a $20-a-day habit, it would automatically go to a $200-a-day habit. That got pretty expensive.

MEGAN.   And he didn't want to do the things we used to do. We used to go dancing twice a week before he left. When he came home, he used to claim he didn't know how anymore.

DARRIN.   "Just dump all that off; it can't be bothering you that much." Obviously they thought I was crazy.

MEGAN.   He'd come home and just sit and stare into space.

TODD.   I couldn't sleep but a couple hours a day, somewhat suicidal, and homicidal, and a bunch of strange things. And so I went to the doctor. I needed something to calm me down because I just shook.

CORY. I had a good friend who got me off the heroin, but he didn't get me off all the drugs. I got my hands on all the marijuana I wanted, and I did all the cocaine and all the LSD I wanted to get because it was readily accepted. It was prevalent—party, individual, whatever.

TODD. I had been an athlete. We started the undefeated football team at my high school, and it stayed that way for 11 years, and I was used to winning. I had gone from 215 pounds to 150...160...something like that. I thinned out a lot during that tour. I went from a lineman, didn't smoke, didn't drink, or do too much anything, into a wiry Marine who was hypervigilant.

DARRIN. I don't think they understood how I felt; I really needed someone to understand. I knew other vets. They knew I was a vet. But we were all told not to talk about it. So it was never brought up, even if you were talking to a vet.

GREEN: TODD C4-C3.

R.MOVER lets JOSH out of the cage and takes him to the enactment area to complement TODD's story. R.MOVER is a doctor giving JOSH an examination.

TODD. So I went in with my papers, and the doctor had seen this before. It was a simple case of...

R.MOVER. Combat fatigue.

TODD. I think they were scared to death of me because I had that look, like I could go through anything. I really was in a lot of pain then.

DARRIN. In the field it was, "Don't mean nothing. Shit happens. Ruck up, soldier." You put it away, and you think it will never come back, but it does—every day of your life.

Vietnamese Chess

RED: *Rook B1-B3.*
R.MOVER hands JOSH a carton of milk which he holds with one arm; with the other, R.MOVER gives him an injection. JOSH becomes suddenly weak.
TODD. So they gave me a couple of injections of Thorazine. Welcome home.
CORY. Then I took my GI Bill and went off to college.
JOSH. Could you please help me open this carton of milk because I can't do it?
CORY. Get up in the morning, about 11:00, roll a joint, watch a little TV, maybe stroll up to the Union and have a little coffee, find somebody to go out and get high with. I even sat in the middle of the Union and did it. It was a common thing.
TODD. Most of the treatment involved some sort of chemical restraint as opposed to a psychologist or more open treatment. Most of it was to inhibit suicidal behavior. The doctors really didn't have much to offer other than drugs.
R.MOVER escorts JOSH back to his cage.
CORY. Before Nam I was just a dumb kid, and after Nam there was a lot of co-dependency. You give me drugs, I give you drugs. You give me sex, I'll give you sex. A lot of co-dependency.
DARRIN. I had some girls that I'd dated, and when they'd come to see me—I couldn't relate to them anymore.
CORY. Any kind of relationship was carnal, a sexual sort of thing, and nothing more than that.
DARRIN. I'd spend a lot of time alone in my apartment painting murals and things on my walls to release— whatever I couldn't say, I'd end up putting it on a wall.
FREEZE—GREEN: Bishop C1-E3; RED: Bishop H2-G3.

Vietnam: Perspectives and Performance

SHEILA. Vietnam became such a personal thing for everybody. I did not go over with a whole bunch of guys; I went by myself with a bunch of strangers and came back with a couple guys I knew, but that whole flight was, what, 18 hours, and we landed in Oakland and we said goodbye and that was it. We went our separate ways.

DAVE. Freedom is something that gives you two directions to take; you can accept the moral imperative or you can reject it. The people I really related to had at some level accepted a moral imperative. Yes, they would kill, but that is neither here nor there. They would do it as politely as possible. They wouldn't mutilate; they'd simply exterminate. There's a difference. [*Nietzsche*]

SHEILA. So it was a personal thing when I left, and it was a personal thing when I came home. There was nobody here who had any idea what I had gone through and that I could talk to.

SUZIE. I was not allowed to go anywhere. I was not allowed to meet any friends except his friends and their wives if he wanted to bring them over. I got pregnant, and he had a difficult time letting me go to the doctor. He didn't trust them.

DAVE. But then there is indeed that set who had taken the other—on the fork in the road, they had taken the dark path: Calley and that crowd. They were criminals, even under those circumstances. They had simply gone too far. There was no excuse for what they did, and it is inexcusable that Lt. Calley is walking the streets today.

SUZIE. He's real protective of his guns—nobody takes his guns. My God, he fought for those guns and he will have his guns! If Commies come over here, he's going to have his guns ready! There are more guns in the house than I would like. I wish we didn't have them at all.

Vietnamese Chess

DAVE. It's the choice of the dark path or the other, and you can enjoy both, and both are equally valid, but one is not acceptable in general circumstances, but they are there, and I understand they are there. I understand Jeffrey Dahmer very well. I understand Charles Manson very well. I could have done it myself with just a very slight shift in decision at that point.

SUZIE. He didn't trust anybody where we lived. In ten months we moved four times.

FREEZE—GREEN: DARRIN G6-G5; RED: Knight D7-C5. G.MOVER takes away SHEILA's alcohol and replaces it with a pen and journal.

DAVE. So, the re-valuing of all values, in terms of immediate reality, a kind of reality which never forces most people living in civilization to confront good and evil. To escape that set of rules and find out the reality that makes them now.

SHEILA. I'm proud of the young men who served there and did their jobs as they were taught to, but sometimes I feel guilty that I came back—I can't say unscarred—because after all I have been scarred. But that's not visible. Only through the practiced eye is it visible.

SUZIE. When we used to go to restaurants, he used to have to sit on the inside so he could look out and see everything at all times.

DAVE. In the war zone, this means you reject the values of pity, kindness, mercy; that you kill and you are alert.

SUZIE. When he would get pissed off, it was nothing for him to say, "I could hurt that person," or, "I could blow him away."

DAVE. And your values are completely revamped.

SHEILA. I probably would have screamed bloody murder if they'd made me spend 30 days on a boat coming back,

– 109 –

but I think in the long run it would have been the best thing that would have happened to us, if they would have brought us back together.

SUZIE. It was in the summertime and we didn't have air conditioning. It was a one-story house. We lived in a place with a deep ravine behind it and there was a lot of shrubbery, trees. No matter how hot it was at night, no matter how hot, every window had to be closed and locked before we went to bed. It was horrible.

SHEILA. I met a guy, a major, who had been shot down during the war, and he said, "Start writing about it." He was right.

GREEN: SHEILA H5-H4.

I started writing, and it has really helped me to try to make real what is swimming around in my head. I can pull it down and put it on paper and it's there. It's helped me to sort through all of it so much better. I think I am more relaxed because of it.

Vietnamese Chess

OPENING POSITIONS

DOWNSTAGE

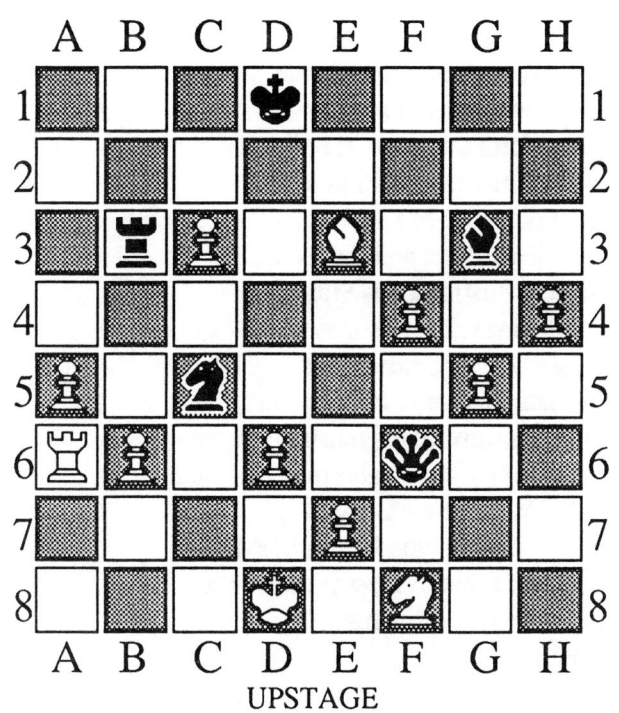

UPSTAGE

MOVES IN THIS SCENE

	RED		GREEN	
1.	Knight	C5-E4	Dave	F4-F3
2.	Knight	E4-D2	Knight	F8-H7
3.	Rook	B3-B4	Matt	A5-A4

Stage is again at halflight and the PAWNS sleep. The MOVERS' chant starts out soft, builds, then ends soft but intense.

CHORUS

MOVERS. Weave the weird dance.
CALLER. Behold the hour
   To utter forth the chant of hell,
   Our sway among mankind to tell,
   The guidance of our power.
MOVERS. Weave the weird dance.
CALLER. Of Justice are we ministers,
   And whosoe'er of men may stand
   Lifting a pure unsullied hand,
   That man no doom of ours incurs,
   And walks thro' all his mortal path
   Untouched by woe, unharmed by wrath.
MOVERS. Weave the weird dance!
CALLER. But if, as yonder man, he hath
   Blood on the hands he strives to hide,
   We stand avengers at his side,
   Decreeing...
ALL. Thou hast wronged the dead:
   We are doom's witnesses to thee.
CALLER. The price of blood, his hands have shed,
   We wring from him.
MOVERS. Weave the weird dance.
CALLER. In life, in death...
ALL. Hard at his side are we![7]

CALLER signals to R.MOVER, who steps onto the board. The crickets are once again heard in the background.

Vietnamese Chess

RED: *Knight C5-E4*
R.MOVER examines the situation and calculates that with the RED Knight in this position, she can attack three of the pieces. Satisfied, she again hovers above TODD. This time she puts her hand over his mouth and mimes slitting his throat. TODD struggles against her as DARRIN wakes up screaming and punching. SUZIE wakes up in shock, wondering what is happening. None of the three are aware of the other two, however. These are, to them, separate events. R.MOVER releases TODD and strolls back to her post.
GREEN: *DAVE F4-F3*
As the lights rise, DAVE is seen sitting in either a Lotus or Half-Lotus position.

Working Pieces

DAVE So here I was, then, between value systems, at a point of freedom, and I threw myself into Buddhism. Life then for me became an adventure. Cause and effect kind of fell by the wayside. I could give a hang about the culture in general. The values had simply become a set of rules which were transparent because a greater reality behind them had suddenly become for me immediate reality.

So life became an adventure. Those things that I had rejected looking at here, I drank up. So, hearing, "Some public officials have just had their throats slit on the beach and the bodies are lying there in the sun decomposing," I would go there and stare at them and look at every exposed artery and vein and pulsation of blood and the coagulation, looking at it as I would in former times admire a rose. So I was at that point, then, trying to absorb everything as a part of myself because that, too, is this ultimate reality. That, too, is God.

So when I leave Vietnam, by anyone's definition I am totally insane. Of course. Anyone who takes pleasure in looking at corpses in the sense of, "This is a set of atoms in a process that is going to occur to me, too," you see; "This is me—this is God."

DAVE resumes his meditation.

MEGAN. When I was pregnant with our first child, I got leg cramps in the middle of the night and just shot out of bed. He didn't know who I was, and he'd react to every sound until he could shake it off and realize where he was. It was frightening. I didn't realize that it had become part of his daily life.

DARRIN. When my mother passed away, I didn't cry.

SUZIE. A lot of times he would just wake me up in the night with his sobbing. He didn't ever want to talk about it, so all I could do was just hold him and let him cry. There wasn't much else I could do. He would either squeeze the life out of me or want me to squeeze the life out of him.

DARRIN. Then it hit me, "Hey, this is your mother, not some guy in the jungle doing his duty on the battlefield." But after one or two times, it's more or less like a numbing effect. You just learn to accept it.

SUZIE. He used to squeeze so tight that I couldn't breath!

DARRIN. You don't really deal with your emotions—you deal with it by shunning your emotions.

MEGAN. This was a man who had loved children—played with all his nieces and nephews, and when our daughter was born I don't think he even held her. I never left her alone with him, 'cause he couldn't deal with it. By the time our son was born, I forced him to, because by that time he wasn't working. For a while, I paid a babysitter while he sat there in the house. I couldn't see doing that anymore.

SUZIE. I didn't know if I was supposed to be his mother or his daughter because I sure didn't feel like his wife. I was his mother in that I was always supposed to take care of him and all his needs, and I was his daughter because he could tell me where I could go, when I could go, and when I could come back, and he could punish me if I did something he didn't want me to do.

MEGAN. Several times I would be in the basement putting laundry away, and I would hear him upstairs walking around calling me. It was almost like a two-year-old, you know, "Mommy where are you?"

I'd come upstairs and say, "I was downstairs."

"Oh well, I couldn't find you." So I had to stay visible for a while.

FREEZE—RED: Knight E4-D2; GREEN: Knight F8-H7; RED: Rook B3-B4.

G.MOVER places the GREEN Knight, then leads JOSH out of his cage in onto the enactment area, then lays him down on the blocks. R.MOVER places the RED Rook, the crosses Row 4 stopping by SHEILA's side. She pauses for a moment to take on SHEILA's persona. As SHEILA begins to speak, R.MOVER plays a nurse to the dying soldier JOSH.

SHEILA. Some days
I can't help remember
when these very young men
without their arms or legs

or half of their faces
looked to me for hope, encouragement,
strength, or peace.
When hidden behind my smile of...
R.MOVER. It'll be okay.
SHEILA. ...was the burden of the lie,
that knew that it wouldn't.
MATT. Take a guy who's had guys' lives in his hands.
R.MOVER begins to leave, but JOSH grabs hold of her hand and makes her stay longer.
SHEILA. Some days
I can't help but remember
reaching out to find a friend,
to hold a hand, to seek a peace,
to find some respite
from war.
MATT. I was doing incredible amounts of medical work in Nam.
SHEILA. Yet even then, I soon did learn
that some would leave
and never come back
from their last fight or their last flight,
but I didn't call in sick in Vietnam,
and I didn't say, "I need a day off
'cause my friend just died."
After all, in Vietnam
somebody's friend died everyday.
JOSH dies, and R.MOVER folds his hands on his chest, but doesn't let go of his hand; she bows her head on his chest.
MATT. I come back to be a nurse, come to find out I have to go back through school to learn how to change bedpans and make beds, when I was out there taking care of massive trauma injuries, inserting IVs, doing

Vietnamese Chess

tracheotomies, doing whatever needed to be done.

SHEILA. Some days
I can't help but remember
I came home to a life
that no longer was real.

R.MOVER's head snaps up from JOSH's chest with an eerie stare, then she rises and leads JOSH back to his cage.

MATT. So I come back and they tell me, "Oh, well you've got to go through the basic CNA course."

SHEILA. Sometimes I tried to explain.

MATT. I said, "Why? I was trained by the best; there is no better...."

SHEILA. Other times I just stayed mute
feeling at first that they wouldn't understand.

MATT. They said, "Well, we realize that, but we need you to go through this course."

SHEILA. Feeling really that they
didn't want to hear,
knowing for sure that they'd
never really know.

MATT. I said, "No, you aren't gonna get any money out of me for that."

DARRIN. I went to see the psychiatrist—I was entitled to it through my benefits. So I went to this man and he asked me some questions, so I told him about some of the problems I was having, and I told him some of the things that happened to me over in Nam. And after I get done talking, he looks right at me and says—and he actually said this, too—he says, "Did you read that in a book?"

SHEILA. And some days
I can't help but remember
realizing that

> I really didn't care
> that the lady down the hall
> was complaining of pain...

DARRIN. As soon as he said it, I got up and walked out, because if I hadn't, there would be one less psychiatrist in the world.

SHEILA. ...and wouldn't get up and walk down the hall.

DARRIN. Maybe I should have stayed.

SHEILA. What right had she to complain of such pain?

DARRIN. "Did you read that in a book?"

SHEILA. A gall bladder after all
was not the same pain
as the kind you get
from shattered legs,
and arms, and souls.[8]

GREEN: MATT A5-A4

MATT. So I got a job in a factory and it was fine—job was fine, everything went smoothly—when I was working by myself. It was working with the other people that was difficult. I was working at one place, and people would start talking about the war, and they didn't know I was a veteran, necessarily. So they'd talk, and it started to bother me. I didn't think they should say anything about it unless they knew something about it, and I'd go off on them. I remember leaving work one day with a dent in my lunchbucket, and the foreman had a hole in his head.

TODD. I wanted to get my energies into something constructive...

TODD & MATT. ...so, I went into construction...

MATT. ...which was my next stop. Worked the next ten years in the construction area, going from job to job to

Vietnamese Chess

job to job. I must have had over sixty jobs. Finally got too old to work in that kind of field, so I swallowed up my pride and went and took the basic nurse's courses and got my certification as a nurse's aide.

CORY.   From '73 to '89, I had to take just about whatever job I could get. I mean I worked everything. I worked in a post office...

TODD.   Construction was okay. It was outdoors. The problem started there with the summer and the heat and the humidity. And I find out not after too long that those kinds of conditions started playing with my mind and I'd have flashbacks.

CORY.   ...I folded clothes in a laundry...

TODD.   Then I worked at the meat packing plant, and that was working in hog blood. And I felt somewhat at home, in a way. It didn't bother me as much as it did the college students that would come in—and leave very quickly—and I can understand that.

CORY.   ...I ran cement crews...

MATT.   After I got certified I worked in the mental health field. I was not allowed to move up in the facility system, and it got pretty boring after three years of it, and I got tired of seeing people come in because they were friends with other people or because they had more influence, walk right up over me. And I'm not blaming them for that, I'm not saying they are bad for this. I'm saying that everything that came down on me as a veteran, as a disabled veteran—I think I got the shitty end of the stick.

CORY.   ...I worked in a junkyard...

MATT.   I worked at that, and all I was allowed to do was put people on and off the toilet, so after three years of it, I'm going, "This is bullshit. I want something better."

TODD.   But I did have some things thrown at me by

employers. I had employers tell me, "Well I've had problems with Vietnam veterans." And they just didn't realize what these guys were dealing with. They were looking at it in the money sense. They weren't looking at it in the sense that they could have helped these guys out.

CORY. ...I weatherized homes for poor people...

TODD. I worked at one place and there was a real stringent security system, armed guards and the whole nine yards. And that bothered me. Then I come to find out that we're making plastic shell casings for the war effort. And that really bothered me.

MATT. So I went back to college, and that didn't work out, because I had been a nurse's aide for three years and I couldn't get a Pell grant, so I just had to go with whatever happened. Ended up being a developmental aide down at the County, but the County's had lots of problems so right now I'm out of a job.

CORY. ...I did construction....

MATT. But I've got a family to support and I don't know what I'm going to do.

G.MOVER holds a bottle of whiskey in front of MATT. He stares at it, then reluctantly takes it from her.

MEGAN. I finally came to the realization that this is not going to be a snap deal. It will be a long, slow process.

Vietnamese Chess

Opening Positions

DOWNSTAGE

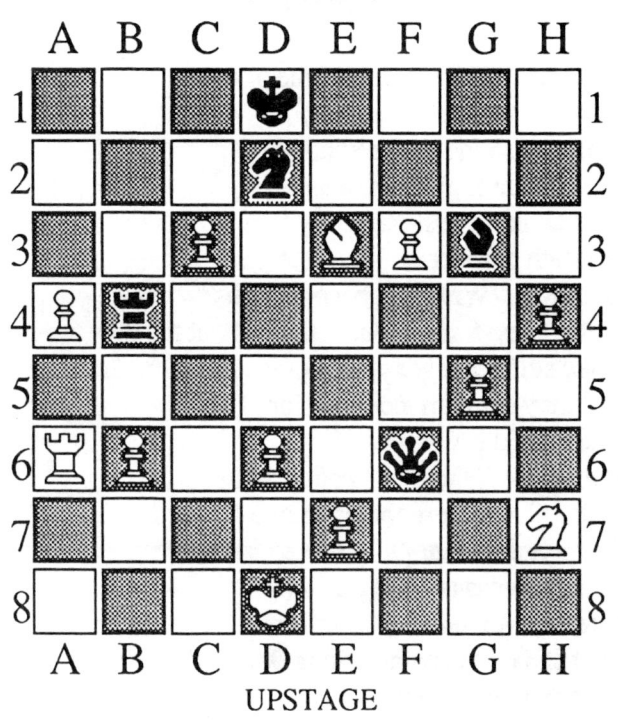

UPSTAGE

Moves in This Scene

	RED		**GREEN**	
1.	Knight	D2-C4	Rook	A6-A5
2.	Knight	C4-D2	Dave	F3-F2
3.	Rook	B4-D4	Dave	F2-F1
4.	Bishop	G3-E1	Dave	F1-H3
5.	Knight	D2-F3	Dave	H3-C8
6.	Queen	F6-E5	Cory	B5-B1

Lights to halflight. DAVE is meditating, MATT is drinking, and the others are asleep.

Chorus

ALL PAWNS.   What will become of us?
CALLER.   There is no answer,
   Only the sound of the wind
   Moving through dead trees.
   And choking dust rising
   Beneath our feet.
ALL PAWNS.   What will become of us?
CALLER.   The furnace burns throughout the day;
   They suffer in agony, as women in labor.
   But they die with the birth, for
   Their child is war.
ALL PAWNS.   What will become of us?
CALLER.   Now these fathers move forward
   To meet their fate
   In open fields and jungle paths
   Strewn with death;
   And call on the name of our God,
   Who will not hear their pleas.
MOVERS.   We pile high the dead
   Into a pale, bleached mountain,
   And swing our bloody bayonets
   Skyward to honor the Victor,
   Who looks through red-rimmed eyes.
CALLER.   And, in time of pain, they die,
   And, somewhere other than home,
   Our names and faces are one.
   Under steel helmets, fear equalizes.

Vietnamese Chess

ALL PAWNS.   One...
PAWNS & MOVERS.   ...is...
CALLER.   One.
ALL PAWNS.   What will become of us?
CALLER.   In the end, Heaven is obscured
   In our agony of pain...
ALL.   ...we know that in victory...
MOVERS.   ...there lies a promise of defeat.[9]

> *The crickets are heard.* CALLER *motions* R.MOVER *onto the board.*
> RED: *Knight D2-C4.*
> R.MOVER *lies down in front of* SUZIE.
> R.MOVER *bolts up, waking* SUZIE, *who reaches to comfort her;* R.MOVER *is startled by the touch, turns with surprise, and starts choking* SUZIE. *As consciousness begins to settle on her, they slowly collapse into a deep hug.*
> GREEN: *Rook A6-A5;* RED: *Knight C4-D2.*

PAWN'S MOVE

DARRIN.   Each of us
   is a can of tomato paste
   and though we may not
   all have the same label
   as we spin thru the air,
   when we land too hard
   or get torn,
   from the outside or within,
   we spill out and
   stain the hands of everyone
   who knew us.[10]

Vietnam: Perspectives and Performance

SHEILA. The "Vietnam Vet"
people instantly conjure
their own picture
in their mind....
Is it ever of
a woman?
huddled...somewhere...
alone
sleeping
trying desperately to shut out the world
that shut her out
or
that disappeared
as she reached out to trust it....
Is it ever
that vision?
that woman?[11]

DAVE comes out of his meditation.

DAVE Most of the people involved in WW II had several things going for them. They had what they considered to be a morally justifiable war. This is why the Holocaust is important and cannot be forgotten: it gives moral justification to the war. Had the Nazis not been bad boys, our government would have had trouble fighting the war. So they come home with a feeling of righteousness...of mission accomplished...of having rid the world of evil.

SHEILA. I was still proud that I served, and I was confused how it had turned out the way it did. It was the first loss, perhaps the most significant loss, I had ever suffered in my entire life.

DAVE At the same time, they come home and they have been involved in the invasion of Europe, either at Normandy or Italy...or the Pacific. And they have been

– 124 –

Vietnamese Chess

exposed to everything I've talked about—this business of confronting their own freedom. And they go through the confusions of that, and then they come back to society and reintegrate, but for their lives, the most significant event was the war. And many in the generation of WW II lost their minds and never got them back. It was such a strong event, such a significant event, that they never got over it. They kept hurtling back toward it.

GREEN: DAVE F3-F2.

Knowing that to be true, and knowing Vietnam happened to me—not by my own choice—I decided, by my own choice, that it would not be the most significant thing in my life.

DARRIN. I was one to do something on the spur of the moment, so one night I decided, "I'm taking off." So I loaded up the car and took off with this girl for Southern California.

RED: Rook B4-D4.

DAVE. At that time Vietnam was still haunting me, and I wanted jungle and I craved heat. So I ended up in Hawaii, which was nice for over a year, but it was part of the same pattern. To escape thinking about what was indeed significant and overwhelming, I needed to do something else significant in its own way.

SUZIE. He had this little room upstairs, and one of the guys said something about it being his bunker, and you know, that was really the way it was. We started to use that little room to smoke in because our son was allergic to cigarette smoke, and we made it into a little sitting room. We had chairs, a TV, that sort of stuff. He had his junk in there. I had my junk in there. Gradually, over a period of time, my junk got moved out to where I had nothing in there. Nothing at all. It was all his.

Vietnam: Perspectives and Performance

DARRIN. That girl stayed with me for a long time. She deserved some kind of medal.

SUZIE. He spent all of his time up there. He came down to work outdoors or to eat meals. He never sat around the dinner table with us when we all sat around. He never sat outside with us when we all sat outside. He stayed up there all the time.

DARRIN. I was working in California, and there was a much higher population of Orientals than there was in Iowa, and with the heat and the palm trees—I guess I was having quite a few flashbacks.

SUZIE. It really affects the kids. I said over the years that however these kids turn out I take responsibility for them, whether it be good or bad, because I was the one who raised them. In a sense that is true; in another, it's not. They picked up a lot of behaviors from him too. The temperaments, reacting in anger—a lot of that they picked up from him.

DAVE. By throwing myself anew into totally foreign situations, I could rediscover myself anew. The people that I know who were involved in WW II, that came back and integrated themselves again into the society, did not have that luxury, and they're still spinning their psychological tires in the mud of Normandy.

DARRIN. Somebody has the wrong turn signal on and you get mad and want to kill them, and you know you can't do that here. Fifteen items in the twelve-item check-out line, and you want to kill them. It's all a combination of all the things that have happened to them—guys that have been fine and successful and everything is fine, and suddenly something will happen and bang! It finally comes back and he snaps.

    GREEN: DAVE F2-F1.

MOVERS. CHECK!

Vietnamese Chess

> *Both MOVERS rush to the RED Queen in order to attack DAVE.*

CALLER. No! *She stops them, commands them to move the Queen back into her former position, then directs them to move the RED Bishop to block the check.*
RED: *Bishop G3-E1.*
DAVE. I refuse to spin my tires in the mud of Vietnam.
GREEN: *DAVE F1-H3; RED: Knight D2-F3.*
DARRIN. This girl was still with me; I have to say she was a tough one.
SUZIE. Our son was about 14—the teen years. There was warfare between those two. I stood between them physically quite often because I didn't want to see it go to fists. There were many times I stood up to my husband. The kid is wrong, but the parent goes way overboard and so the parent is wrong, too.
DARRIN. But she started to tire of it, of a person who was always armed, who would do unexpected things. She came home one time—I was in a flashback—I was sitting in the top of an oak tree watching her, and we lived on a private road, and it was kind of scary up there—the nearest neighbor was probably 500 meters away. So I went up in this tree and was watching.
SUZIE. I was at the sink one day and our son was screaming. I looked out outside, and my husband had him by the throat and was beating his head against the wall.
DARRIN. I watched her talk to the dog, and then go into the house and try to find me, and finally I come flying out of the tree...
SUZIE. I went out there...
DARRIN & SUZIE. ...and [she/I] told [me/him], "Don't

you ever do that again!..."
SUZIE. ...and never touch him again or I will call the authorities myself. I mean the poor kid had marks on his head from it, and you could plainly see them, too! He has never done it again.
DAVE. I don't reject it. I don't forget it. It is simply another chapter, as opposed to *the* book of my life. And it will not be any more exciting or meaningful than any other chapter. That is my goal.
GREEN: DAVE H3-C8.
SHEILA. I still am extremely gunshy. I can't stand the Fourth of July. Car exhausts bother me. Helicopters going over my head bother me. I mean, I become instantly aware. You just tune in immediately. It doesn't seem to go away. The phone rings and I can't—it just jars me terribly and I don't know why. I can't get over that. It's conditioning, I guess. While you're there, every day is filled with tension—filled to the maximum. I thank God for those who have been able to overcome it. I still haven't overcome it. Vietnam is still with me. I think there isn't a day that passes that I don't think of Vietnam. It comes back to me.

FREEZE—RED: Queen F6-E5.

R.MOVER lets JOSH out of the cage and leads him to the enactment area. They will recreate MEGAN's story. He is given the shotgun and sits on the blocks facing the audience with the gun across his legs. R.MOVER "piddles" behind him at the start.

MEGAN. It was in the summertime, and he was outside and told me he was going inside to tape a movie. He went in, and I piddled around outside for a while.
CORY. When the Iran Hostage Crisis occurred—that

Vietnamese Chess

triggered something I hadn't dealt with before. It was different than nightmares and different from depression.
MEGAN. I went back in and I realized that he was sitting there with the TV on, but he wasn't watching it. I think he said something to make me realize he must be in a flashback.
TODD. I realized after the Iran Hostage situation where the Vietnam vet stood in the minds of the United States.
CORY. So, I took off into the timber and stayed there— I'd leave Friday night and come back on Monday.
MEGAN. He was sitting on a chair, and he had his gun on the chair.
TODD. It's nothing against those people; I'm glad they got out alive.
CORY. You pitch your tent and you build a fire and don't do anything, just sit there, drink.
TODD. But then I compare how we came back—how I came back—I mean, there's no comparison. I've tried the psychiatrists.
MEGAN. I called a psychiatrist he'd been seeing, and the psychiatrist tried to talk to him on the phone, but he didn't even hear him.
TODD. There's no one out there that understands what it was like to be in Vietnam.
MEGAN. The doctor said he would call the authorities for me because he knew that I couldn't get him out of the flashback on my own.
CORY. I'd spend weekends driving, too. I'd get on the interstate and I'd just go for twenty hours or so, turn around, and drive back twenty hours. I'd stay out all night. I wouldn't come home.
MEGAN. He also told me to get all the guns out of the house. I had to go right in front of him to do this, but I got all the guns and shells out of there and into the trunk

of the car.
CORY. Just sleep in the van, sleep in the garage, just wouldn't come in the house.
TODD. There is no one out there to whom I can communicate what I saw and what I thought and how I felt.
MEGAN. Then I went back to the living room and was trying to talk to him, but he did not hear me or acknowledge me.
CORY. In '79, that's when I felt really ignored, unappreciated...
MEGAN. He just kept saying...
JOSH. I'm all by myself, and it's dark.
TODD. There is no one—but another vet.
CORY. ...forgotten.
MEGAN. He did look my way a couple of times, but I didn't know if he saw me or the VC.

CORY cocks the gun.

CORY. I felt deserving of something because of my time spent in defense of the country.
MEGAN. He shot the gun and threw the gun on the floor. I ran and picked up that gun, ran to the car, and took off.

CORY begins a trek toward B1.

CORY. When the Hostages came home and they even rolled out the red carpet for them. They were welcomed home.

As he reaches B1, he raises the gun to his head. CALLER urgently gestures to TODD, who suddenly becomes aware of CORY and bolts up to stop him from killing himself.

TODD. Welcome home.

Vietnamese Chess

Opening Positions

DOWNSTAGE

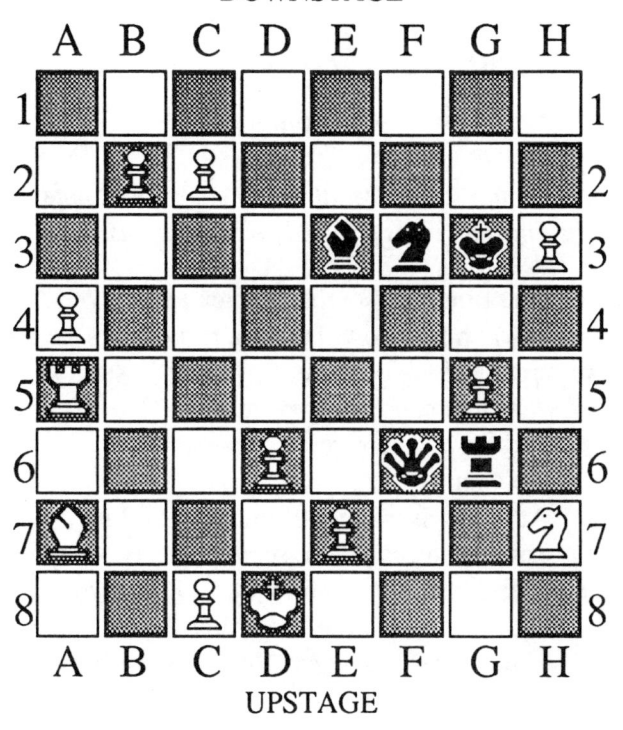

[Chess board diagram, 8×8 grid with columns A–H and rows 1–8]

UPSTAGE

Moves in This Scene

Sheila	H3-H1
Matt	A4-A1
Suzie	D6-D1; D1-H1

Lights rise on the chorus at their posts.

Chorus

MOVERS. Behold!
CALLER. What wrongs they endure.[12]

Moving Pieces

CORY and TODD are talking to each other; note the time lapse has affected piece positions.

CORY. One time we were in an area and they called us up—this is at night; now, I'm on a reconnaissance team; we're supposed to be quiet. Nobody's supposed to know we're there. And they tell us, "The B-52s are going to arc-light where you guys are at."
TODD. Holy shit.
CORY. And this is at night, and I'm thinking, "We're going to die." Unless you've seen the holes—they leave some hellacious craters. And they told us to go find the lowest depression in the area, lay down, open our mouths, and cover our ears. So, we knew where this creek was at, so we took off running through the jungle in the dark, and again, we're supposed to be a *recon* team, right? Nobody's supposed to know we are there. And we finally get there, and they call us up and say, "The mission has been aborted." Well, now we've completely compromised everything we've ever done. And I'm thinking, "Yep, this is real good." That was one of the many times I thought, "I'm gonna die from one of our own bullets."
GREEN: SHEILA H3-D1.
SHEILA. I was talking to a marriage counselor. My

marriage was falling apart. And I was with him and all of a sudden visions started popping into my head, and I don't remember exactly how the conversation went on, but he said, "What do you mean? Why are you talking about Vietnam?" And so I told him that I had been in Vietnam, and it occurred to me that he was the first person that I had mentioned it to in so many years. It was the first time anybody had ever asked me about it, and I was just going crazy wanting to mention it.

SHEILA crosses the board and sits on a stool by CORY and TODD.

MATT. The first time I came down to the support group.

MEGAN. There was an article in the paper about the symptoms of PTSD that nailed him right down the line. I didn't even know that it existed, but apparently I'm not too far behind the times on that. There are so many doctors that say it doesn't exist. PTSD can happen to anybody. It's not just the veterans.

MATT. Well, the very first time I came down, I just drove right on by.

MEGAN. I wish he had started going to those meetings a long time ago. It is obvious that he can't talk to me about it. At least he can go there and talk to the other vets.

GREEN: MATT A4-A3.

MATT. The second time I parked the car across the street for about a half-hour.

MEGAN. They encourage each other not to drink, not to do drugs—whatever is their biggest weakness.

GREEN: MATT A3-A2.

MATT. The third time I made it as far as the door, and I almost went in, but I just wasn't ready.

MEGAN. He has finally gotten to the point where, if he feels like he needs a drink, he will call one of the guys in the group, which to me is a tremendous step forward.

GREEN: MATT A2-A1.

MATT. The fourth time I finally went all the way, and it was scary as hell. And I sat down and I looked around at all these guys, and knew quite a few of them, and they started talking about this and that, about the war and problems, and then I started talking about my problems, and I just let it all out right then and there, all of it. And that was stuff I'd never talked about before, stuff I was carrying around for almost twenty years.

SHEILA. If I had known then what I know now about Agent Orange, I would have drank more scotch and less water.

MATT. According to the military, there was nothing seriously wrong with me. They gave me a physical and said, "Okay, you're out of the service." Since then we lost our son, a first-term stillborn, and there was no explanation for his death other than he had something wrong with is respiratory system.

SHEILA. Several years ago, my shoulder, my arm, and down to my hand and everything kept tingling and going numb, and so I went to my doctor and he gave me some pills. Muscle relaxants. They thought it was a pinched nerve. Then I discovered that the area I was in was one of the most heavily sprayed with Agent Orange, and I thought, "Well, it could be that, too."

MATT. My oldest son, living today, had a tumor in his chest cavity when he was 7 years old the size of a small football. There's no explanation for that.

SHEILA. It turned out to be cancer. Lucky for me the treatments were successful.

MATT. I receive $145 a month—20%—10% for high blood pressure and 10% for my knee. You can, depending on your rating, get up to $1500 a month, but you have to be really messed up to get that. As far as

Vietnamese Chess

money goes, there's not much support. You have to fight and argue and fight and argue every step of the way. It's really sad that the veteran's arch nemesis is the Veterans Administration. You think, "Well they should be fighting for us, not against us." But that's what it is, a fight, and it shouldn't be that way, but when you've got the government cutting funds....

SUZIE. At one point he brought home a list of different symptoms of Post Traumatic Stress Disorder and it was a pretty good long list. He told me to read this. He said, "This is incredible. This is me!" I read through that list and I thought, "Yeah, this is just an excuse for him to be the asshole that he was."

MEGAN. At that time they just wanted to label everybody as alcoholics. He went to the VA for two years before they gave him 10% disability. It was not for PTSD, but it was the best we could do because if there is one thing those guys don't want to do it's wait around.

SUZIE. The VA's answer was, "You have to deal with the alcoholism and then we'll see if you have PTSD." I've even had friends who've said this, and it doesn't seem right. They pushed alcohol at these guys, and now they're saying, "Well, you deal with your alcoholism and then we'll see if you have PTSD!"

MEGAN. For example, he had to be there for a 9:00 appointment with a psychologist. They said, "Well, we don't have you scheduled for that time. It was supposed to be two weeks ago!" On our paper it said the 19th, and they had us down for the 9th. Thank goodness I learned to keep everything the VA sends me, and I had that letter with us.

SUZIE. Now, they are finally saying that alcoholism may be a symptom of the trauma. But they also say that this trauma could have occurred prior to his service, which

Vietnam: Perspectives and Performance

means that he can't receive compensation for PTSD. According to them, it's not war-related.

MATT.   A lot of our guys would call, "Corpsman up!" when they needed help. And the North Vietnamese, being so cagey and so smart and such a devoted, dedicated enemy, so close in the fighting and the confusion, liked to yell, "Corpsman up!" too, to get these guys up and moving around. In fact, we know of one instance where they walked a corpsman right into a hole, and there were 4 or 5 bad guys in there, and the mutilation to that kid was just unbelievable. With that strategy, how the hell was this going to get any better?

SHEILA.   There was a process called triage, and the philosophy behind triage is to do the most good for the most people—

TODD.   I lost a corpsman one time. Boy, he was good. He came up to me and said...

JOSH.   I don't want to go this time. I'll go next time, I've gone every other time.

TODD.   He said...

JOSH.   I've got a bad feeling about this.

They wait for TODD to continue, but he locks up. To fill the silence, SHEILA returns to her story until TODD cuts her off again.

SHEILA.   And there was one Surgeon General who would walk around and make the decision of who went into the operating room first. And that was a bad job; nobody liked pulling that shift because it was playing God—

TODD.   And I said, "You've got to go." And of course he never came back. He was smart, he was good-looking, his dad was a minister, his sister was a concert pianist, which doesn't make him any better than anyone else, but he was a bright kid. That haunts me to this day, that I made him go. I had to. I think about that kid every day. Every day. How do you resolve that?—when you think you're responsible. Somehow that boy just symbolized all of them, you know? It's how you just like someone. I knew that one. I knew his name. Death is there, but every once in a while there's that one that's different than all the rest. And why that one affects you where the next one didn't—somehow one or two stay in your mind and stay there forever.

TODD is pretty shaken up and SHEILA stands behind him with her hands on his shoulders.

SHEILA. So they made those choices and also decided which could be done under local anesthetic. And we did a tremendous amount of stuff under local. When I look back and think of some of the things we did under local—it's almost criminal, what we put these guys through. But when the operating rooms were jammed up, it was the best you could do. And this was the healthiest population we were working with; these are strong young guys, and they can get both legs blown off, and they can wait; you clamp off the blood vessels, and let the guy who was shot in the chest or the belly go first. We used a tremendous amount of blood. The transfusions were amazing. If a guy used 20 units of blood, it was hardly worth a comment at supper that night. If somebody used 30 or 40, you might say he used a lot of blood. But if you got to the hospital, your chances of surviving were pretty good.

During MATT's story, DARRIN pulls out a handgun, studies it for a while, and cocks it.

MATT. About five years ago a good friend of mine who is also a Vietnam veteran, had experienced a divorce—and problems over and beyond that, couple of OWIs and what have you—and went home from work and killed himself. And we didn't think anything of it until

Vietnam: Perspectives and Performance

Monday when he didn't come up for work. And I was having some hellish dreams, and every time I had a dream, we'd both be in it, and I'd be carrying him through the jungle and telling him that it'd be all right and that we were going to make it.
DARRIN puts the barrel in his mouth.
But he never had a head on him in the dreams—he never had a head.
DARRIN stops himself and shoves the gun away, takes his medication, and lies down.
And I must have had that 10 or 12 times until I finally worked through it.

MEGAN. I wish there was a magic wand you could wave and say, "You're all well." But that is impossible.

SUZIE. These men are trying to deal with their thoughts and emotions and everything that happened to them during Vietnam and since they've come back. Then there's the wives who deal with the men, plus the children, the family life, the home life. The men are trying to deal with their emotions now some 20 years later, and they have all they can do to handle that. The '90s expect us to be everything to everybody.

MEGAN. It is going to be a long process. Some heal to the point where they can deal with themselves and society. Others—I don't know. I'm not sure any of them will reach a "curing" point.

SUZIE. I think the women of the '50s had it better.

MEGAN. There are a lot of things that I have gone through that no one else would. I'd try to tell what was happening to somebody else, and they'd say, "Get rid of the stupid ass! I wouldn't put up with that. Get rid of him!" They don't understand. Other people just don't understand how things can be fine and then one thing can happen to trigger it and he would just blow. I feel like

Vietnamese Chess

it's my responsibility if everything goes wrong or if nothing goes wrong.
GREEN: SUZIE D6-D5.
G.MOVER moves onto the board and stands beside SUZIE as her daughter.

SUZIE. I found all these suicide letters all over, and I went into an absolute panic, which is exactly what he wanted to happen. I made some phone calls and found out where he was at and that he was okay. Our daughter wanted to talk to him. I didn't want to see him at that time, but she was very adamant that she wanted to say something to him. I was so proud of that little girl! She read every one of those letters while I was making phone calls trying to find him. I didn't even read them all. I took her to see him. She walked in with those suicide letters and she threw them on the table and she said...

G.MOVER. Dad, do you have any idea how I felt when I read these letters? I'll tell you what. If you commit suicide, someday I'm going to die, and whether I meet up with you in heaven or in hell—I'm going to kill your ass again!
GREEN: SUZIE D5-D4.

SUZIE. She was just crying her little heart out.

MEGAN. It will be 25 years in December if I have anything to say about it or he does.
GREEN: SUZIE D4-D3.

SUZIE. It was just like a lightbulb went off that said, "You don't have to live with him!"

MEGAN. He doesn't want to split up for any reason. He is very proud that with all these other Vietnam vets, their marriages always fell apart, but we have been married for years and his family was still together. He's always been real strong on that point. You know—home and family.

>   GREEN: SUZIE D3-D2.
>
> SUZIE. I got out my little calculator and figured out how much I was making and how much I could make working full time and about what it would cost me to live, and found that I might be able to do it. This started on a Friday; Saturday I got out my calculator, and Sunday I made my decision.
>
>   GREEN: SUZIE D2-D1.
>   *SUZIE kneels down and G.MOVER kneels beside her.*
>
> When I left, the kids all left too. They followed me. I had always said that he and I would never get a divorce. Never. One of us might kill the other one, but we would never get a divorce. I really believed that. So, the kids have always heard me say this. Then when they heard me tell them I was leaving—and at that time I didn't even talk divorce—it was just leaving. I needed to escape. Every one of those kids said...
>
> G.MOVER. Mom, we told you you should have left a long time ago.
>
> SUZIE. It made them stop and do some thinking.
>   *G.MOVER walks with SUZIE to H1. They hug, then G.MOVER exits the board. SUZIE sits cross-legged in the square.*
>
> MEGAN. When he asked me to marry him, he hadn't been out of the service too long. He said, "I don't have anything, just me." He gave me this ring that he'd gotten over there. A little ring, maybe worth a dollar. And that was my engagement ring. And I still have it. It's my ring. A lot of people really don't understand the circumstances of living with a vet. My own family doesn't understand. I know they get upset because he doesn't do what they think he ought to do, but I'm the one living there and not them. I figure it's between us.

Vietnamese Chess

CORY. I went on R&R and I had no feelings whatsoever for anyone. I can remember the girls—I had no interest in them. A good friend of mine and I, we went out partying, and you could look up girls in a book, girls with numbers, and you could get anything you want, and have sent up to your room, and that's what we did. And I wanted to kill the girl. It took everything I had not to do it, and she could understand it. She had seen it before. I can remember talking to her and drinking with her, and don't think I ever went to bed with her—

G.MOVER lets JOSH out of the cage as MATT crosses to the enactment area.

MATT. We had a guy—he was one of the homeliest kids I ever saw. He had no waist—his legs came right up to his shoulders. He had a terrible complexion. But that guy was tough. Tough. When they wanted to go one of those long range jobs, never complained a bit. Probably never had a girlfriend in his life, right? Goes to Tai Pei for R&R, and he comes back and he is in love, right? He's got pictures of this girl and all this stuff. About three days later he comes up to me and he says...

JOSH. Doc, I got the clap and I got it bad.

MATT. This guy was sick. 105° temperature. He was sick as hell. So I loaded him up with penicillin, and of course you don't put any of this on his records. So he gets transferred down to Phu Bai, and later I run into him again. And, I say, "How ya doin'?" And he says...

JOSH. Great! I got another R&R!

MATT. I said, "Where ya goin'?"

JOSH. I'm going back to Tai Pei.

MATT. And so I say, "Well take care of yourself this time, will ya?" And so he goes down there. About ten days later there's a knock on my door. Same girl, same bar, same price, same problem. That kid was shy,

Vietnam: Perspectives and Performance

though. He said...
JOSH. I don't care. I had the greatest time of my life. I'd do it again. I don't care.
MATT. When I first got there I used to hear guys say that, and I would judge them quite harshly. But after you are there ten days or a few weeks, you'd say, "Did you have a good time?"
JOSH. I had a great time, Doc.

MATT crosses back to the group.

MATT. And you'd do whatever for them and that's that. They lived for R&R—or the more appropriate term for R&R as I called it was I&I, Intoxication and Intercourse. That's what they did. More power to them, as far as I'm concerned. Because those guys, they deserved whatever pleasure they could find.

Chorus

CALLER.   O Strength of God,
ALL.   Slow art thou and still
   Yet failest never!
R.MOVER.   For all is vain...
MOVERS.   The pulse of the hearth...
ALL.   The plot of the brain...
G.MOVER.   That striveth beyond the laws that live.
CALLER.   And is thy faith so much to give?
   Is it so hard a thing to see...
ALL.   That the Spirit of God, whate'er it be...
CALLER.   The Law that abides and changes not...
ALL.   Ages long...
CALLER.   The Eternal and Nature-born,
   These things be strong?
GR.MOVER.   Happy he, on the weary sea
   Who hath fled the tempest and won the haven.
R.MOVER.   Happy whoso hath risen, free,
   Above his striving.
CALLER.   For strangely graven
   Is the orb of life.
ALL.   And men in their millions float and flow
   And seethe with a million hopes as leaven.
G.MOVER.   And they win their Will...
R.MOVER.   Or they miss their Will...
MOVERS.   And the hopes are dead or are pined for still.
ALL.   But whoe'er can know
   As the days long go...
CALLER.   That To Live is happy...
ALL.   Hath found his Heaven![13]

DARRIN wakes from a nightmare.

PAWN'S GAME

SHEILA. Even now,
After twenty years,
I still feel
abandoned and forgotten
Uncounted,
Unnumbered.
Forgotten, silenced and cast away
for over two decades
and now I can't deal with
the newly kindled interest.
"Did you see Sixty Minutes?"
and I want to scream and
rip off their faces:
Where was your interest
and empathy over the past
twenty years?...
Buried out back
with your old dead dog?[14]

MEGAN. I got in an argument with a woman the other day about Kent State.

CORY. Kill them all!

MEGAN. I used to think that, too. At the time, I thought they should line those protesters up against the wall and shoot them down. On some things, I'm not so forgiving.

SUZIE leaves H1 and joins MEGAN.

SUZIE. When the rumblings started, the protests, it was never, "Bring our boys home—we want to stop them from being killed." It was, "Bring our boys home—we don't want them to kill the Vietnamese anymore!" It wasn't supporting the troops or the families.

Vietnamese Chess

MEGAN. You could shoot Jane Fonda down in front of me and I'd clap.
CORY. I'd shoot her.
SHEILA. I thought she was a damned fool. Purely that. I thought it was an interesting way to get a lot of attention.
SUZIE. They're not going to accept her apology. She has no problems. She's been married and remarried and made her money off the war, and then she cussed it! I remember living through it and thinking, "Lady, do you even know what you're protesting against?" If she wanted to protest, why didn't she go to Washington to see our politicians? The guys over there were just doing what they were told.
MEGAN. But I have changed my mind about Kent State though.
SHEILA. I read an article, an editorial, that said that the courage was the same for those going to Canada as those going to Vietnam. That's a lie. That's a disgusting thing to say. Every once in a while I read that, and I wonder what I'm going to write back to him.
TODD. I have nothing against those who went to Canada. *This is a playful argument. TODD knows he's riled her; SHEILA is earnest about what she's saying; but the exchange maintains a non-threatening quality.*
SHEILA. I know that we make difficult choices, that those who went to Canada went through trying times. I know the ones who went to Vietnam had extremely trying times.
TODD. I have a feeling that there were some who were indeed cowards, who went out of fear. Well, then they themselves knew well enough to relieve us of putting up with their fear. They wouldn't have been helpful in that situation. So they did the world a favor.

Vietnam: Perspectives and Performance

SHEILA.   But to equate courage—to say the courage is equal—is a vile, despicable thing to say, because for these guys who faced that every day as opposed to those who sat in Vancouver—there's a difference in the quality of courage involved and it wasn't right for him to say that. Who ever heard of the Battle of Windsor Tunnel?

TODD.   Then there are those who for some moral imperative felt that it was wrong to go to Vietnam. Fine. I'd never argue against that.

SHEILA.   Or facing those pastries in Montreal everyday? I suppose that was tough.

TODD.   There were about fifty guys in our company, and I'd say at least five of them were from Iowa. I think that has a lot to do with the Midwestern values we were brought up with.

DAVE gets up from his square and begins to move toward the group.

DAVE   Some people thought it was fine as long as it was, "Not my boy. You send the neighbor kid, you send the darkie from Chicago, you send the redneck from Alabama, that's fine."

MATT.   Some of the Black guys liked to tell stories of what their life was before—I found that a lot of them didn't have anything back home.

SHEILA.   I had always kind of looked down on Southern Whites because of their redneck attitudes, their racial attitudes, and I felt that way until I got to Vietnam and I was with these guys.

DAVE   But if you're white and you're college material, "Don't send my boy." That's the way it was. It's no wonder that there was a disproportionate number of minorities over there.

MATT.   They came out of the Projects and they were Marines trying to get a life.

Vietnamese Chess

SHEILA. They are the toughest, the most courageous bunch of guys I ever saw, the backbone of the US military. What an education I got! I have heard people say that the US military is made up of a bunch of "good old boys." Well, you be damn proud that the military is made up of "good old boys."

MATT. They were pretty hardy individuals. They didn't take the rough conditions as bad as some of the people.

DAVE. And to look at it in a different light, for every one that didn't go over there or that went to Canada, a veteran took one of their places. That is, regrettably, a fact. There's no way to cut that.

DAVE joins the group.

SHEILA. Tet was the turning point. I didn't know it at the time, but history tells us. It was the cruncher politically. One photograph—any good PR person can tell you the power of one good photograph. And the photograph of the seal of the Embassy on the United States torn down, and the sappers on the ground—it was a devastating political view. And that whole summer the whole political scene changed with the riots in Chicago at the Democratic convention. Those were monstrous happenings in the States at that time, and that all kind of came off the events of Tet. And that's when the peace movement politically descends. There was a tremendous political upheaval going on, all swung off that war. When they write *The Rise and Fall of the United States of America*, the Vietnam War will be the focal point of that. I really feel our world is so different since that war occurred.

MATT. There's an interesting point between the students today, whose only real concern is the long-range plan, and our generation. The students today are thinking, "Okay, where will I be in 5 years? In 10 years?" Back

Vietnam: Perspectives and Performance

then, unless someone had a specific draft deferment or political pull, long-range plans were ridiculous.

SHEILA. All we knew about Vietnam is what we saw on TV and had read in the papers. There were no good books. There was no one who spoke the language. There was no information on the culture. Vietnam was a skull-and-crossbones on the map. The only evidence that the place existed at all was the combat on the six o'clock news. That was Vietnam.

MATT. So there was a lot of immediacy, here-and-now, flower-power, and get-your-kicks-while-you-can as opposed to postpone, delay and look-toward-the-future, because there could very possibly have been no tomorrow for college students, should Vietnam catch up with them.

SHEILA. Television was television—cheap thrills at the expense of the public. Newspapers and magazines worked much better, but they had the same problem the nation in general had. The Vietnamese did not exist in our consciousness.

MATT. Everywhere you looked there was the reality, the presence of military involvement. The National Guards and the ROTCs were more prevalent on many campuses than they are now. You just don't see that today. You don't have a military reality of American forces imposed upon you day-by-day as we as the college generation had it imposed on us. It was very strange, very trying.

SHEILA. They were simply these things out in the jungle that we did not see. They were unknown. And we molded them "gooks." They were dehumanized. And it is easy enough to do that when you have no knowledge of the people.

MATT. It was a Revolution, a people's war. They talk about the 300 people killed in My Lai, but the news

– 148 –

Vietnamese Chess

media conveniently forget to mention the 3000 that were butchered in Hue by the Viet Cong. They don't bring that up. You ask any group of people, "Who has heard of My Lai?" Hands will go up all over. You ask, "Who has heard of Hue?" No hands at all.

CORY.   My first fire fight, five VC came across a rice paddy and none of them were over 18, and some of them were lucky to be 14. And they managed to kill one of our corporals. He only had twenty some days to get out of there, to go home. I didn't know him really well, but I had talked to that guy every day since I got there. They went down in a tremendous amount of fire. That's when I first learned the devastation that can be inflicted with an M-14 at 100 yards, and when I opened up, it mangled them. Split one of the kids right in two, basically.

TODD.   I think that a lot of them must have been 15 or 16 years old that I saw in uniform. Fifteen or 16 fighting against us 18 or 19. That was the story. It was fought by children.

CORY.   I can still remember the face; it looked so young, and it was only half there, half of it was completely gone. That's stuck in my mind forever. Then they put those bodies on mules and drove them around; it was like a parade for them. Trophies. I couldn't hardly stand to look at them. Who would even do that? What American would take a .30 caliber carbine with five guys and come across a team of Marines with an M-60? I know I wouldn't do that.

DAVE   We had a Vietnamese boy living with us on the compound. I always called him Squeak. A team had found him a few years before, and he was a legal resident of the base, and I don't know if he ever did get back here or not. I think he was ten when they found him. What they told me—of course you don't know how much of it is truth or legend or whatever—but what it was is they were near some area, and apparently he'd recognized some Vietnamese people, VC, who had killed off the people in his village, and he went off and stole a gun and went out and killed them. He brought the gun back, told them exactly what he'd done, and that ended that. He had no desire to touch a gun again. But he lived with us, and he could play cards and cuss. He was the best card player, pool player. He was quite the kid. He was fun to have around.

DARRIN. I got close to a lot of the kids who had been orphaned early on, and I had boxing gloves and things sent from the States to recreate with them. And they had hopes and dreams, most of them, of getting out of Vietnam. The young wanted to come to the United States and asked a lot of questions. And a lot of them knew a lot about the United States; they had studied it. Most of the men were off fighting. The kids I saw were 10 or 12 years old.

SHEILA. I think the main one that sticks in my mind, I think he had to be an Amerasian because he had blond hair and blue eyes. I think that little guy's still in my heart. I hope somebody got him out of there.

DARRIN. There was a little ten-year-old that I was trying to adopt. He was at the orphanage, and he'd shine shoes, do errands, get me lunch. And I decided to adopt him. There was a lot of paperwork, a lot of red tape. I thought everything was going along fine; it was close to the end of my tour. It was a hard decision to make. I was nineteen years old and I was trying to adopt a ten-year-old kid. And we talked about it quite a lot, and he was anxious. He had to stay at the orphanage at night, and that made me uneasy because the VC liked to pick up kids 10 to 13. It was kinda hard for a 19-year-old....

Vietnamese Chess

So a guy and I were coming back to the base one night at 3:00 in the morning, and in the light we saw a figure go by and it wasn't going very fast. So we just froze. Joe asked me, "Do you see what I see?"

I said, "Yeah."

So he went to one side and I went to the other. We could tell that he had grenades strapped to his body. So I came around behind him, and I had my knife drawn, and I just grasped for the neck and slit the throat. Joe screamed, "Did he pull it? Did he pull any?"—of the grenade pins. I didn't know. And somebody flipped the light on, and it was my son.

I freaked out. They had to wrestle me into one of the rooms and lock me up. I just went berserk. I wanted to shoot anything that moved.

The VC nabbed him out of the orphanage. I requested an autopsy, and the doctor said that the VC had put so much heroin in his body that he would have been dead in a half hour anyway.

MEGAN. I think I want people to know that these guys were 18, 19, 20 years old. Look at them today! Do they have enough self-confidence to be in protection of one country? I don't think so!

DARRIN. When I came home, I was drinking heavily. I was about three sheets to the wind when I got on the plane. Well, one guy sitting across from us, out of the blue says, "You guys from Vietnam? Just got back from Vietnam?"

I said, "Yeah."

"Oh, a bunch of baby-killers."

I almost killed the guy.

MEGAN. He doesn't come to church with me. Ever since that war. It's like he's given up on God. It really worries me.

DARRIN takes some of his pills and lies down to sleep. He doesn't awaken for the rest of the play.

MATT.   When I was in Nam I carried my rosary and a photograph of my wife.

MEGAN.   I've tried I don't know how many times to get him to go with me, but it just doesn't interest him anymore. He wasn't like that before.

MATT.   I remember services in the field and the chaplains handing out rosaries. He'd take a vote, and whatever denomination had the most people present, he'd do the services that way. To have that in the middle of a war zone—those were some of the most powerful sermons I have ever experienced. They took on a whole new meaning.

TODD.   We had this chaplain, and he and I got in this fight one time about something and he says, "Fuck you!"

And I said, "Hey, you're a chaplain. You shouldn't talk like that."

And he said, "OK...Fuck *Thee!*"

Chorus

The PAWNS are frozen. CALLER steps down from her podium and goes to the edge of the board. She takes a strengthening breath, steps onto the playing field, and approaches DARRIN.

CALLER. Alas! I pity him. Without a friend,
Without a fellow-sufferer, left alone,
Deprived of all the mutual joys that flow
From sweet society—distempered too!
How can he bear it? O unhappy race
Of mortal man! doomed to an endless round
Of sorrows, and immeasurable woe![15]
   She approaches the group.
   Alas, ye generations of men, how mere a shadow do I count your life! Where, where is the mortal who wins more of happiness than just the seeming, and, after the semblance, a falling away? Thine is a fate that warns me to call no earthly creature blest. But now whose story is more grievous in men's ears? Who is a more wretched captive to fierce plagues and troubles with all his life reversed?[16]
   She gestures to DARRIN.
   Behold into what a stormy sea of dread trouble he hath come! Therefore, while our eyes wait to see the destined final day, we must call no one happy who is of mortal race, until he hath crossed life's border, free from pain.[17]

   CALLER returns to her podium.

ENDGAME?

TODD.   There is still a lot of survival guilt. Enormous. I am really surprised I am still alive.

SUZIE.   I would like him to be better. I regard it as a mental illness. If I could change anything he would be out of his own little hell hole. To me it seems like each one of them is in their own little hell hole and each one is floundering around in there and not being quite able to grasp anything to pull themselves out. It can't be fun for them—it hasn't been for me. We have no idea what they are seeing in their minds from Vietnam.

TODD.   The support group really helps because you get the feeling that you're out there but you are not alone. The isolation factor of the PTSD puts you behind walls, and you're in this vacuum of aloneness that makes psychotic thought possible. Sometimes it appears that there is no way out.

SUZIE.   I feel like the government stole my happiness by messing up my husband and all the Vietnam veterans. They came home in shame. Nobody ever told them, "You did a good job. You did what you were supposed to do." Instead they were spit on, laughed at, and made to feel like they were idiots.

MEGAN.   There were five guys from our area that went into the Marine Corp. His best friend was one of them. They all came back and everyone of them is screwed up today. One is on his fifth marriage.

SUZIE.   I think he thinks that I just breezed through it all, that it was just fun and games, a joke—and it wasn't.

MEGAN.   His best friend—they're still married but he's had all kinds of drinking problems. One of them is somewhere in a cabin in Minnesota. One of them came

Vietnamese Chess

home and protested the war—Vietnam Veterans Against the War. He didn't get married, but he had problems. He did finally get help and was a lot better. I don't have much contact with the rest of them anymore.

SUZIE.   I've talked to gals who've met guys after it all and don't know them before. I don't know how they do it. At least I have some point of reference to see the true person he should have been or could have been.

CORY.   I've been to Washington, but I've never seen that damn wall, and I don't care if I ever do, and I'll tell you why.

MATT.   The war has no significance. The dead do. Their names are there. That signifies. The significance of the war is in the Wall, where we lost 58,000 and their names are there.

CORY.   When I came back from Nam, I went to look up some friends of mine, and I found out they both had been killed. That's enough for me.

MATT.   They're there, and for what? Nothing. It's a descent into God-knows-what and ascent out of it in which we walk away and hope we never have to go back.

CORY.   I don't want to go to that wall and come across the name of somebody else I knew. I'd just as soon keep thinking they are alive somewhere. I just don't want to see it.

Lights come up on JOSH writing in his cage.

JOSH.   Dear America,
They tell me that the war is over and that you have turned your attention to other things. They tell me that there is a black wall in Washington bearing the names of the dead and that Americans leave mementos there for those who died. They tell me that my name is on that wall. Is that true? Am I dead in your mind? They tell me so many things that I don't know what to believe anymore.

I did not die. But many of the men that you left behind have died. Of wounds or an illness of the body that was easy to see. The sickness of the soul that so often set in was harder to detect. Yet, I am not afraid to join those fallen POWs. After all these years of hoping, of believing that the next dawn would begin my journey home; at least death holds the real promise that I will, at last, be free of this place.

But, death is a two-edged sword for me. For my death would extinguish the memory of those who died here before me. They live now only in my mind. If I should join them today, no one would ever know that they were here—that they kept the faith beyond measure. Only for them will I go on and try to remember for one more day that I am an American soldier bound by duty and honor. For them, I will try to believe that tomorrow's dawn will begin our journey home.

TODD. There is the hope in the back of a lot of families' minds that loved ones who are not accounted for are alive. They are the victims of anyone who wants to use it to his own political advantage. It's a chime they ring when they want a little attention from a certain level of society. It's too bad, really.

JOSH. If I am to remain here forgotten—forever—and if I am destined to join the brave prisoners who have died before me, I am more comforted than you. For I know that I will fall on ground that has already been made sacred by their valor and that I will be held in soil that has already been made hallow by their sacrifice. So, do not shed your tears for me. Place your mementos at your own doorstep. For the greater loss is not in my passing here, but in your own lingering silence there.

They can bruise my body and torture my soul. They can strip me of my dignity and deny me my humanity.

Vietnamese Chess

They can cripple my mind and crush my spirit. But only you, America, can break my heart. Only you.[18]

SHEILA.   I hate that POW/MIA flag. All that black. But I'll see it on every church and on every courthouse because of those people that we left in Vietnam and in Korea and in World War II.... Because of those people, I'll see to it that that damn black flag is flying everywhere across this country!

Through the concluding pages, all PAWNS (except CORY, MEGAN, and DARRIN) will, after their last line, walk up to Row 8, step off the back of the board, and exit to the left.

MATT.   I'm getting to the point where it doesn't affect me as much. It used to be everything. I realized not too long ago what I was doing. I was relating everything to Vietnam. Everything. I could look at a door frame and the door, and I'd think, "Well, in Vietnam there would have been beads hanging down instead." Or, I'd be driving along looking at the treeline and think, "Well, in Vietnam, the treeline would look like this." I related everything back to my life in Vietnam. Now I'm getting to the point where I can do other things.

SHEILA.   I'm okay as long as I'm doing something constructive. I'm not the type to sit around and worry, so what I can do about it is go and make a little piece of it better. As long as I am able to do that, I'm okay.

MATT.   I get a lot of satisfaction now helping out with Special Olympics. To be out there with those kids and help them—they have so much fun. They really appreciate it, you can see it in their eyes. It's one of the most satisfying things I've ever been involved with.

DAVE.   I didn't expect that it would act against me and it has. I lost five years of my life. Career-wise I could have been a very naive and more well-paid, middle-aged

Vietnam: Perspectives and Performance

man, had I not suffered at war. But I lost two years in the military, and I'd say a full five years trying to get over it. No real resentment—I didn't allow myself to resent it.

CORY. And it's still there in a lot of ways, it's still there, but it's getting to where it's less and less everyday—where I'm not so dependent upon people for my pleasure and my feelings, and the group has brought that out. I can go in there every Wednesday night and cry my eyes out as long as I get something accomplished during the week.

TODD. But there's a fallback with that, too. Sometimes you can become so dependent that that's it for you. And you just can't go with that. There are other things in life. That's why I always stress getting the guys involved in other things besides vet things. You've got to get out there in the world, and you've got to get going. But with a lot of them there's still that fear.

DAVE But I do have a feeling that in this society, any attempt to communicate other than the most superficial—I wouldn't feel surprised to say ideas, but information—is rejected.

SHEILA. Every veteran has a story to tell, and every story will be unique and amazing, even if he sat in a desk in Saigon for eleven months. Just to glean the thoughts and feelings and perspectives of someone who lived in a war zone—that means something.

DAVE I would say that that is my case: to know, and to not communicate. And to know it's hopeless.

Exit DAVE.

SHEILA. There is not a veteran alive that doesn't have something important to say, and I am so glad that people are starting to ask, and listen, and learn.

Exit SHEILA.

Vietnamese Chess

SUZIE. I think I want people to understand that every Nam vet out there who does crazy things or is a hermit or is anti-social in some way or another, that these guys were kids when they went over and did something that no other age has been put through before.

MATT. All these guys that come up to you and say, "You Goddamn Vietnam veterans, why don't you stop crying like babies and whining about the war and get your act together." And I guess I agree to a point, but they don't understand that until the past six to ten years, a lot of veterans never had that opportunity. They had nowhere to go except themselves. But now, with the group and everything else—Desert Storm, all that—people are starting to say, you know, "Hey, what happened to you guys?" I think people are finally starting to understand.

Exit MATT.

SUZIE. If they could project onto these middle-aged men with pot bellies and greying hair, project a scared teenager onto them, and see that when they went to do a man's job they came back old from seeing things that none of us ever want to see.

Exit SUZIE. TODD gets up, starts to walk up the board, then stops and turns back to the audience.

TODD. One thing about surviving it, and I know a lot of vets don't want to hear this, but it's got to start with us. I know that the whole country has to join in to heal us, because they have to heal, too, about Vietnam, but we vets have to make that first move. We have to take the first step and start cleaning ourselves up first. Then we can reach out and help everyone else to heal, and that'll help us to heal even more. But the vet can't wait for it to happen. He has to start it himself. Welcome Home.

TODD exits.

Epilogue

CALLER.   If you are able,
save for them a place
inside of you
and save one backward glance
when you are leaving
for the places they can
no longer go.
G.MOVER. Be not ashamed to say
you loved them...
R.MOVER. Though you may
or may not have always.
ALL.   Take what they have left
and what they have taught you...
CALLER.   With their dying...
ALL.   And keep it with your own.
CALLER.   And in that time
when men decide and feel safe
to call the war insane,
take one moment to embrace...
ALL.   Those gentle heroes...
CALLER.   You left behind.[19]

Lights go down on the CALLER and MOVERS, leaving the remaining PAWNS in half-light, then slowly fade to black.

END OF PLAY

Vietnamese Chess

WORKS CITED

1. From *Agamemnon* in *Greek Drama*, Vol. 1, pp. 181-182.
2. A letter from *Dear America*, pp. 258-259.
3. From *The Bacchae* in *Greek Drama*, Vol. 2, p. 266.
4. Ibid. p. 240.
5. From *Agamemnon* in *Greek Drama*, Vol. 1, pp. 199-200.
6. From *Choephori* in *Greek Drama*, Vol. 1, pp. 230-2.
7. From *Eumenides* in *Greek Drama*, Vol. 1, pp. 281-282.
8. "Some Days" in *Visions*, pp. 89-93.
9. "The Victors" in *Dear America*, p. 166.
10. "Letters from Pleiku" in *Dear America*, p. 174.
11. "The Vietnam Veteran" in *Visions*, p. 94.
12. From *Prometheus Bound* in *Greek Drama*, Vol. 1, pp. 157.
13. From *The Bacchae* in *Greek Drama*, Vol. 2, p. 261.
14. "Even Now" in *Visions*, p. 131.
15. From *Philoctetes* in *Greek Drama*, Vol. 1, p. 562.
16. From *Oedipus the King* in *Greek Drama*, Vol. 1, p. 408.
17. Ibid p. 417.
18. "Dear America" from Task Force Omega.
19. "Untitled" in *Dear America*, p. 29.

PROPERTY LIST

1 Chess Set	1 Wine Bottle
1 Wine Glass	2 Liquor Bottles
1 Deck of Cards	1 Sketch pad and pen
1 Calculator	1 Latchhook Set
1 Photo Album	1 Notebook and pen
1 String of Rosary Beads	1 Book
1 Newspaper	2 Syringes
1 Plastic Bag of "Cocaine"	1 Hashpipe
2 Bottles of Pills	1 Shotgun
1 Fashion Magazine	1 Handgun
1 Checkbook with Bills	1 Carton of Milk

Vietnam: Perspectives and Performance

Afterword

"You portrayed my mother perfectly while honoring my father—now it's my turn to tell my story...."
—A child of a Vietnam veteran

We hope that these scripts have offered an insight into the experiences of Vietnam veterans and their families. There are, of course, many other related issues which were not focused upon in these productions, including the perspectives of children, parents, and siblings of Vietnam veterans, of POW/MIAs, of the problems relating to Agent Orange, and a multitude of others. In addition to the veterans community, the contemporary views of protesters, military advisors, or political figures during that period could also be explored. It is often easier to find material about those veterans who are stuggling to come to terms with the war. Those who have "gotten over it" are not always a vocal faction. Their stories, as well as their methods of coping, would be excellent material for a thorough investigation.

There are those who adamantly proclaim that Vietnam was a good idea gone bad, and others just as loudly berate it as a terrible mistake from Day One. Both views share at least one common view—something went wrong. As a nation, then, it seems that our responsibility is to recognize these mistakes, not run from them, if for no other purpose than to ensure that those same errors do not occur again.

The legacy of Vietnam is a painful yet crucial part of understanding our national heritage and metaphorically of understanding the human condition. There is a wealth of insight and perspective still available. All we need to do is reach out and grasp it.

About the Authors

PHYLLIS CARLIN received her Ph.D in Communication from Southern Illinois University–Carbondale in 1976. She teaches ethnographic research, language and social interaction, oral history, and performance studies at UNI. Her research areas are personal narrative, performance in everyday life, oral history in cultural/community identity, and genres of women's discourse.

CHRIS ELLSBURY received his BA in Communication Studies from the University of Northern Iowa in 1993. He is currently working toward an MA in English Literature at UNI. His current research involves tracing the literary tradition of Hamlet.

MARILYN SHAW received her MA in Communication Studies from the University of Northern Iowa in 1986, where she teaches courses in communication, performance studies, and literature. Her current research is in Native American folklore.

JENNIFER TERRY received her BA in Communication Studies from the University of Northern Iowa in 1993, and she is currently working toward an MA in Communication Studies at UNI. Her current research is in performance in everyday life and the personal narratives of tombstones.

About the Association for Textual Study and Production

The Association for Textual Study and Production was founded by members of the University of Northern Iowa Department of English Language and Literature in 1993. Its purpose is to cultivate and sponsor publications and the study of literary texts.